Deaf Education
in America

Deaf Education in America

Voices of Children From Inclusion Settings

Janet Cerney

Gallaudet University Press
Washington, D.C.

Gallaudet University Press
Washington, D.C. 20002
http://gupress.gallaudet.edu

Library of Congress Cataloging-in-Publication Data
Cerney, Janet
    Deaf education in America: voices of children from inclusion settings / Janet Cerney.
      p. cm.
    Includes bibliographical references.
    ISBN: 978-1-56368-362-6 (alk. paper)
    1. Deaf children—Education—United States. 2. Inclusive education—United States.
3. Deaf students—United States. I. Title.
    HV2551.C38 2007
    371.91'20973—dc22   2007023058

To my three precious children Anna, Tasha, and Alosha, who gave me the passion to understand your deaf child's view of deaf education in America.

That all men are alike is exactly what society would like to hear. It considers actual or imagined differences as stigmas indicating that not enough has yet been done; that something has still been left outside its machinery, not quite determined by its totality.

—Adorno, 1974

Contents

Preface

As SCHOOLS are increasingly moving toward integrating deaf and hard of hearing children, it is important for educators, parents, and policymakers to recognize the complexity of this issue. A deeper look at the influences of communication and relationship building, as well as their interaction, may help to identify for whom and under what circumstances integration is successful. Improved decision making by those involved in placement and implementation is only possible when the perceived benefits and risks associated with the integration of deaf and hard of hearing children are identified and carefully weighed.

Since the communicative needs of deaf students are unlike those of other groups of students with disabilities, their plight cannot simply be an extension of the overall movement toward integration of students with disabilities. Instead, their fundamental human right to language must be examined, studied, and planned for in their daily lived experiences in school. In considering the quality of communication and relationship building in the learning environments for deaf students, it is useful to gain an understanding of the nature of the real-life communicative relationships of deaf students in inclusive settings. This information can be gleaned only through the perspectives of deaf students exposed to inclusive learning environments and the professionals who give them access to the voices beyond them.

The interviews contained in this volume are the culmination of a qualitative research study investigating the quality of relationship building and communication in the integrated learning environments of deaf students. Since the research in educational interpreting has been scant, this study originated as an attempt to gain a deeper understanding of the perspectives of students and interpreters on their relationships and other factors that influence success in an interpreted educational environment. A secondary goal was to gain knowledge of the barriers that deaf students face in accessing communication in integrated learning environments, as well as the support structures they need to succeed.

The data gathered for this text comes from interviews with 10 deaf students, 5 deaf adults, 10 educational interpreters, 4 regular education teachers, and 2 deaf education teachers involved in the integrated experience of deaf students. Interviewing seemed particularly important for the population of deaf students in that it allowed them to communicate through their native language, American Sign Language (ASL), while removing the possible barrier of not understanding written English surveys or forms. This method also allowed a clearer understanding of the perspectives of these individuals while offering an opportunity to explore the themes embedded within their stories.

A foundation for designing effective interviews was drawn from the ideas of Rubin and Rubin (1995) in their book *Qualitative Interviewing: The Art of Hearing Data*. From this perspective, qualitative interviewers listen to people as they describe their lives, based on their understanding of the world. A narrower form of qualitative interviewing is evaluation interviews, a tool the researcher uses in discovering the views of those interviewed in the successes and failures of a program or project. Another form of qualitative interviewing is cultural interviews. This tool allows the interviewer to ask about shared understandings, standards of value, and mutual expectations (Rubin & Rubin, 1995). My goal was to combine elements of evaluation interviews with cultural interviews to gain dual insight into the cultural and evaluative perspectives of environments for deaf students

At the beginning of each interview, each participant was asked to identify his or her language preference for the interview: spoken English or American Sign Language. Nine of the deaf students chose ASL as their preferred mode of communication for the interview. One student (identified as Leslie) chose to conduct the interview in spoken English. All participants were interviewed directly through ASL or spoken English by a bilingual researcher fluent in both languages. Interviews conducted in ASL were videotaped and transcribed by a certified interpreter. Interviews conducted in spoken English were tape recorded and transcribed by a native English transcriber.

A substantial decision in planning for interviews seemed to be the choice of *whom* to interview. The goal was not in conformity, but in the complexities of the viewpoints and their places of divergence and inter-section. Initially, it seemed that the greatest opportunity for understanding would come from choosing pairs: education interpreters with the children they service. But this would be asking interpreters to violate their code of ethics by disclosing information about a specific client. Therefore, this study focused on the perspectives of educational interpreters collectively, rather than on a single comparison with a specific child.

Most interviews took place in the homes of those interviewed. This was important for three reasons. First, the participant was able to reflect on his or her experiences in a non-threatening and comfortable environment. Second, since signs can be read at a distance, this provided the most protective and confidential environment for deaf participants. Third, this freed the participant to think with more latitude of his or her whole lived experiences, rather that being influenced to focus on one context.

Glossary

For the purpose of building a common understanding, the following terms are defined as follows:

Auditory/Oral Programs: Programs based on the principle that most deaf and hard of hearing children can be taught to listen and speak with early intervention and consistent training to develop their hearing potential (Oberkotter Foundation, 2003).

Integration: The placement of deaf children into hearing classrooms for part or all of their education. This term will encompass the terms *inclusion* and *mainstreaming*.

Mainstreaming: The practice of moving children from their special education classes for part of the day and placing them in general education classes (Knight & Swanwick, 1997; Stone, 1994). The range of options may include attending only nonessential curriculum activities (lunch, recess) or attending selected classes.

Schools for the Deaf: State schools that exclusively educate deaf and hard of hearing students. Though these schools historically have served as residential schools, area students often commute as day students. Most schools for the deaf currently have a policy that supports ASL or total communication (using sign and voice) in teaching deaf students.

Self-Contained Classroom: A classroom for deaf and hard of hearing students within a public school. It typically serves as the place of instruction with a teacher of the deaf. It is also home base for interpreters and students moving back and forth between mainstreaming.

Resource Room: Any room that a student may go to in order to receive instruction outside of the regular classroom. A resource room may be used for multiple purposes and with students of various disabilities.

Inclusion: The process of placing students with disabilities in the same schools, classes, or programs as their typically developing peers and providing them with necessary support services. Supporters of full inclusion believe that placing children with disabilities full time in regular classrooms with nondisabled children gives all children equal access to learning experiences (Bunch, 1994). The generic goal of inclusion seems to be to provide all children with equitable opportunities for a successful education (Knight & Swanwick, 1997; Rafferty et al., 2003).

Inclusion–Team Teaching: Students with disabilities are placed in inclusive settings, while a special education teacher jointly teaches the class with the regular education teacher.

Reverse Inclusion: A relatively small group of nondisabled students (20%–40%) is added to a specialized program for children with disabilities.

Continuum of Placements: The most common placements follow a continuum, depending on the amount of time spent in regular education classrooms.

Schools for the Deaf	Self Contained Classrooms	Mainstreaming	Inclusion

Continuum of Placements

Under the generic interpretation of "least restrictive environment," the students would be moved as far to the right as possible, placing them with hearing children to the greatest extent possible. However, many voices in the discourse of deaf education argue that the further to the right students move, the *more* restrictive their communicative and learning environments. They instead support the belief that a truly "least restrictive environment" would be the furthest placement to the left—schools for the deaf (Cohen, 1994c; Leigh, 1994; McCartney, 1994; Ramsey, 1994; Schildroth & Hotto, 1997; Stinson & Lang, 1994; Stone, 1994).

Part 1

Deaf Education in America

The Social Side of Learning

1

AS THE MORNING BELL RINGS, public schools are filled with the sounds of voices. Students shout to their friends, and teachers greet each other. Halls burst with the latest news in the bustle of the moment. Chatting students drift through classroom doors to a place of learning. The social scene, alive and brimming within the prattle, discourse, and gossip of the day, begins to jostle with the tide of formal knowledge building.

Behind classroom doors, discourse changes as conversations are guided to a renewed focus on learning. Teachers question and students respond. Students question and teachers respond. Voices of debate, collaboration, and purposeful thinking come together in discourse as students engage in the language of learning.

Deaf students who attend public schools experience a very different world from their hearing counterparts. It's as though they walk and live behind a soundproof wall that serves as a complete barrier to the messages floating around them. Where the hearing peer is lavished with language and discourse, the deaf student is often deprived of the words and the content, as well as the relationships that these voices represent. The phenomena are only slightly altered by the involvement of an interpreter, who attempts to funnel all of the voices into a single channel of access.

Imagine for a moment what it would be like to be deaf in a public school. You cannot hear what people say, but you struggle with trying to read lips—even though only 25% of speech is visible on the lips (Vesey & Wilson, 2003). You cannot hear your own voice—but you struggle with trying to form words recognizable only to hearing people. You may wish for a best friend to hang out with or to tell you hidden secrets, but only adults share your language.

Deafness affects more than a person's ability to hear, it has the potential of influencing human communication in a profound way (Aymard & Winstanley, 1992). The deprivation of communication in the learning environments of deaf students has been a growing concern to many in the field of deaf education. The focus represented in the literature surrounding deaf education strikes at the heart of academic achievement—access to language. Articles, research studies, and lived experience stories have been published describing the ramifications of enforced placement in inclusion or mainstream settings, where a language barrier leads to deprivation of language and deprivation of social contacts. Oscar Cohen, a leader in the field of deaf education, reports that "contrary to the claims of those who champion 'normalization,' placement in a school setting that lacks appropriate communication with peers and adults creates an abnormal and impoverished milieu" (Cohen, 1994b, p. 35). Lawrence Siegel raises similar concerns in *The Educational & Communication Needs of Deaf and Hard of Hearing Children*: "It does not seem possible that there are children in America at the beginning of this millennium" who are placed in an educational system that "does not provide quality, communication-based educational programs" (Siegel, 2001, p. 5).

Learning as a Social Experience

Nostalgic pictures of early American classrooms provide a glimpse of an educational system and philosophy that is becoming more and more distant. The hallmark of the traditional classroom was an active teacher, who maintained control of the pace, sequence, and content of the lesson through direct instruction. While research regarding direct instruction suggests it is an effective means of teaching factual content, there is increasing concern in the literature that it does not effectively foster higher-order cognitive skills, such as reasoning and problem solving. Now this input model, heavily dominated by direct instruction, is taking a backseat to collaboration, interaction, and relationship building—a new perspective emerging from a social constructivist theoretical foundation.

The major theoretical contributions to the social constructivist perspective were developed in the 1920s and 1930s by Vygotsky and his contributors (Palinscsar, 1998). The constructive perspectives are rooted in the dual orientations of psychology and socioculturalism. Vygotsky proposed that learning awakens a "variety of internal developmental processes that are able to operate only when the child is interacting with people in his environment and with his peers" (Vygotsky, 1978, p. 90). In further support of this perspective, Vygotsky writes that from a sociocultural perspective, learning and development take place in socially and culturally shaped contexts. It is within these contexts that teaching and learning occur and where learning is viewed as culturally integrated—a social, motivational, emotional, and identity processes (Palinscsar 1998).

Piaget also contributed to our knowledge of learning through his theory of sociocognitive conflict—a social interaction that creates a contradiction between the learner's understandings and the learner's experiences (Piaget, 1985). Piaget suggests that the social exchanges between children are more likely to lead to cognitive development, compared to the exchanges between children and adults. This observation was premised on the belief that among age peers there is mutual control over the interaction.

Though the ideas of the social constructivist theory surfaced nearly a century ago, the contemporary interest in creating classrooms as social learning environments is a fairly recent endeavor. The recent decade has witnessed a "sociocultural revolution" (Voss, Wiley, & Carretero, 1995, p. 156), with a focus on cognitive science theories supporting the acquisition of intellectual skills through social interaction. Much of the recent research on teaching and learning has been conducted from a postmodern constructivist perspective. This research is unified by a rejection of the view that the locus of knowledge is in the individual; instead, it grasps the belief that learning and understanding are inherently social and regards cultural activities and tools (including language) as integral to conceptual development (Palinscsar, 1998). Recent educational reform efforts encourage students to assume a more active role in learning—explaining their ideas to one another, discussing disagreements, and cooperating in the solution of complex problems. Meanwhile, teachers participate in the design of these contexts and the facilitation of this kind of activity (Resnick, et al., 1993). All these notions, based on social constructivist perspectives, have had an enormous impact on the culture of schools.

Social Learning and the Integration of Deaf Students Into the Classroom

When learning is redefined as an interdependence of the social and individual processes in the co-construction of knowledge (John-Steiner & Mahn, 1996), the role of communication and relationship building is crucial.

Many believe that the recorded difficulties that deaf children experience in learning and developing social skills are only exacerbated in regular classrooms (Afzali-Nomani, 1995). While a hearing child is often exposed to a rich environment of multiple direct relationships within the classroom, the deaf child's experiences are limited to the interpretations of one person—the interpreter. Though the effect of limited direct communication and relationship building on the achievement of deaf children is not clear, we can assume that is does have some effect.

This assumption is further supported by the literature. For example, Bell et al. (1985) studied conversation tasks and determined that children working with peers showed more cognitive growth than children working alone. However, the children who derived the most from peer learning were *actively engaged* in problem-solving activities and not merely observing a more advanced peer (Bell, Grossen, & Perret-Clermont, 1995). This finding is important to understanding the experiences of deaf children, since deaf children involved in collaborative activities with hearing children may not equally participate in the activity; instead they often become more passive observers. Forman and Kraker (1985) also suggested that verbal interaction is the key to co-construction and cognitive change. In their study of seventh-grade students involved in spatial relations prediction tasks, they found that cognitive conflict might not be enough if there is insufficient verbal interaction or if the social structure permits passive participation (Forman & Kraker, 1985).

The social role in learning is widely recognized by supporters of the sociocultural theory. But while a hearing child is often exposed to a rich environment of multiple direct relationships both inside and outside of the classroom, the deaf child's experiences are often limited to the interpretations of one person. The extent to which this unnatural restriction affects the education of a deaf child is still unknown. Yes, the child may be able to function in this environment, but can the child thrive and reach his or her educational potential? It would seem that the significant language barrier that prohibits direct communication would also limit the deaf child's ability to maximize his or her learning within this environment.

The issue of language and social deprivation for deaf children goes beyond the classroom walls. While hearing children are exposed to communicative relationships with parents, siblings, grandparents, neighbors, and others outside of the home, many deaf children are deprived of those relationships. Families of deaf children often never learn to sign, and instead rely on lipreading and gestures (Gallaudet Research Institute, January 2003). Too many times, deaf children arrive at school age with very limited language ability—leaving school as the place for language learning to occur, including conversational skills (Griffith, Johnson, & Dastoli, 1985).

To what degree does language deprivation affect learning? Some researchers feel that brain development requires a bath of language—including adventurous words, grandmother and grandfather language, and religious and philosophical terms—all of which require elaborate syntax (Bly, 1996). When deaf children are isolated from language at home and at school, the ramifications of language deprivation may be broad and overreaching.

What are the long-term effects of social isolation and language deprivation? Researchers have gained knowledge in studying extreme cases such as Genie, a child isolated from social and language exposure until age 13 (Curtiss, 1977). Their conclusions support the critical age theory that language learning must take place by a certain time or the learning will not happen fully. A study of deaf signers of ASL who were first exposed to ASL at different ages found that children exposed to ASL from birth mastered both word order and morphology, children exposed to ASL between the ages of 4–6 made frequent errors in morphology, and those who were exposed to ASL after puberty used whole-word signs with no morphological structure (Newport, 2001).

Though researchers have studied black and white cases of total language acquisition from zero language input, there is currently little information available concerning more mild cases of language deprivation. However, some teachers from residential schools for the deaf have noted that students who come from inclusion settings typically lack latitude in conceptualization and vocabulary in comparison to deaf students who have benefited from multiple direct communicative relationships with peers and teachers. Experts at the National Center on Deafness also concur that lack of communication reinforcement may harm the ability of deaf and hard of hearing students to acquire and retain language. In addition, they state that due to lack of strong communication skills, deaf students may fail to acquire language completely and, therefore, may have weak literacy skills (2002).

Alternatives in Learning Environments

Many in the field of deaf education point to deaf schools as the answer to the problem of creating rich communicative and socially active learning environments for deaf students. While deaf schools certainly do provide an option that is attractive to many deaf students, others would have to move far from home to explore such an option—making it an undesirable choice. So the question remains, "Is there a way to make integrated environments suitable and appropriate for deaf students?"

One alternative is the model of co-teaching deaf and hearing students together (Kluwin, 1999; Jimenez-Sanchez & Antia, 1999; Kreimeyer, Crooke, Drye, Egbert, & Klein, 2000). A random sample of comparatively equal numbers of deaf/hard of hearing and hearing students in grades four through eight revealed that the students did not feel socially isolated, or lonely, and their self-images were no poorer than those of their hearing age peers (Kluwin, 1999). However, it was noted that issues of cost, time, and achievement gap serve as deterrents for many school districts. Therefore, a critical need exists for innovative ideas in addressing the academic, social, and communicative needs of deaf students.

Historical and Cultural Influences in Deaf Education

2

Historical and Cultural Context in the Education of Deaf Students

CONCEPTUALIZING THE ISSUES SURROUNDING the education of deaf students involves understanding the historical context of deaf education, the political platforms that have developed, and the current forces that are impacting deaf education today. The subject of deaf education is highly charged both emotionally and politically (Zapien, 1998). The answers are neither perfect nor simple.

For centuries the education of deaf children has been polarized into two main camps, the manualists (those who sign) and the oralists (those who rely on speech and speechreading) (Zapien, 1998). A third camp has more recently been added—supporters of cued speech (those who use a sound-based visual communication system). But the clash between manualists and oralists reaches deep into history and deep into the emotions and experiences of those who have been educated under their slogans. So that we can gain sensitivity toward the plight of deaf students and not repeat the mistakes of our past, it seems important that educators, parents, and administrators understand the history behind the controversy and recognize the juncture between feelings and facts.

A Glimpse Into History

On April 15, 1817, a motley group of twelve deaf students entered the Connecticut Asylum for the Education and Instruction of Deaf and Dumb Persons. They ranged in age from 12 to 51 years old. Some students were from prominent New England families, while others came from the unrestrained and spirited deaf community at Martha's Vineyard. Their walk through the open doors signified the beginning of formal deaf education in America, a history that has sparked one of the most radical and controversial educational wars of all time.

This bold beginning to American deaf education was laid by the friendship and camaraderie of two men: Thomas Hopkins Gallaudet, a hearing minister, and his chosen counterpart Laurent Clerc, a deaf Frenchman. It was through their joined effort that the school thrived. Culturally, the school was deaf friendly, embracing the visual language of its students. Laurent Clerc was a successful deaf role model, teaching classes, as well as providing training to other teachers. His partnership with Thomas Hopkins Gallaudet seems to have been one of equality, as Gallaudet wrote of his great respect for Clerc. Together they traveled, securing financial help for the school and building a successful learning environment for deaf students. Interestingly, both Gallaudet and Clerc married women from the first graduating class.

The prompt and spectacular success of the Connecticut Asylum brought enthusiasm to the burgeoning field of deaf education (Sacks, 1989). By 1820, plans to educate deaf Americans were being made around the country. As new residential schools for the deaf began to spring up, many deaf students discovered language and a new cultural family after living for years in communicative isolation within hearing communities. Within the walls of these schools, the older deaf children would pass down to younger generations of children the cultural attribute that made deaf Americans a distinct subculture within America—sign language (Lane, 1992).

This early academic culture was marked by a prevalent respect for deaf people as teachers and school leaders. Hearing administrators tended to approach the students from a loving but paternalistic viewpoint, consistent with other educational institutions of that time (Van Cleve, 1993). Sign language flourished, and the brightest deaf students were later recruited as teachers. By 1858, deaf teachers accounted for a full 40.8% of the total teaching force in schools for the deaf (Gannon, 1981).

The first recorded attempt in America of educating deaf and hearing children together surfaced in 1852, when a hearing teacher from the Hartford school became concerned for the education of the younger children ages four to seven. The opening of Mr. Bartlett's Family School for Young Deaf-Mute Children signified the beginning of both inclusion and the education of younger deaf students. Bartlett saw mutual benefit by educating deaf and hearing children together—the hearing students provided incentive for the deaf pupils to speak, while the deaf students provided incentive for the hearing students to learn sign language and develop interpreting skills (Gannon, 1981).

Frederick Knapp also attempted inclusion in 1877, when he admitted deaf pupils to his private school in Baltimore. However, his perspective was far more condescending, as he believed that "the more deaf students socialized with hearing students, the less they would notice their defect" (Gannon, 1981, p. 14). In Knapp's school, hearing children were forbidden to sign to deaf children, in an attempt to keep them from reminding deaf students of their affliction. If a hearing or deaf child were caught signing, he or she was forced to wear gloves to signify "punishment and stupidity" (Gannon, 1981, p. 14).

Although American Sign Language enjoyed widespread support through the first half of the nineteenth century, by mid-century, a new method of teaching deaf children, oralism, began to emerge. This method emphasized lipreading and speech and prohibited the use of signs. It gained international support during a meeting of administrators and teachers in Milan, Italy, in 1880. Though this deaf educators' conference drew participants from France, Italy, America, and various other European countries, it was dominated by the oral teachers from France and Italy. The American delegation included Thomas Hopkins Gallaudet's two sons, Edward Miner Gallaudet (the president of Gallaudet College) and Thomas Gallaudet, who both spoke strongly in support of sign language. The oralist agenda dominated, though, and in the end a motion passed to pledge full support to this "method of articulation"—giving international approval to the idea that deaf children should be forced to communicate without signs (Van Cleve & Crouch, 1989). This resolution was published and distributed to all known schools and programs for deaf students (Bremner, 1996). Its existence sparked the beginning of the international suppression of the communication rights of deaf children.

Even though the American delegation strongly opposed the resolutions, the Milan conference created a buzz within American borders, promoted by sensationalized headlines and politicians who did not understand the cultural identity of the deaf community. The well-known Alexander Graham Bell, as well as doctors, hearing parents, and their professional organizations, called for a total ban on sign language, believing the use of signs was a barrier to deaf people learning speech and becoming normal citizens.

The highly vocal Alexander Graham Bell led the charge to abolish sign language, becoming the "most feared enemy of the American Deaf" (Van Cleve & Crouch, 1989, p. 77). He firmly believed that deaf people were "a defective race of human beings" and a "great calamity to the world" (Gannon, 1981, p. 10). Ironically, both his mother and wife were deaf, and Bell himself was a fluent signer. In 1883, he presented a paper to the National Academy of Science in New Haven, Connecticut, "Upon the Formation of a Deaf Variety of the Human Race." His presentation supposed that since we can modify breeds of animals by careful selection, it should be possible similarly to modify the varieties of the human race (Gannon, 1981). Based on his assumption that deaf marriages lead to deaf children, he found deaf residential schools, deaf community events, socializations, and the hiring of deaf teachers disturbing and intolerable in nature because they could lead to intermarriage.

Initially, the residential schools were skeptical of Bell's efforts. Though many teachers, including Edward Miner Gallaudet, found value in teaching some speech techniques to hard of hearing students, they were mostly interested in teaching content to students through signs instead of wasting endless hours on speechreading drills. Bell and other oralists realized that in order to have a significant effect on these institutions, they would have to organize. Bell used his influence to enlist the National Education Association in his struggle against sign language. Ultimately, he was able to use their lobbying powers to win the hearts of politicians and public school teachers for the oralist movement. By 1920, despite deaf students' need to use signs to communicate and build a knowledge of the world, 80% of deaf students were educated without using any signs (Van Cleve & Crouch, 1989).

The effect on deaf education and the deaf community was devastating. The ban on sign language had a great impact on the deaf teachers, who had once been welcomed. As oralism spread, deaf teachers were removed from their positions, some without any compensation, and were quickly replaced by hearing teachers who did not know sign but were well versed on the drills of speech training. The ranks of deaf teachers shrank rapidly, as most administrators would not risk their positions by hiring a deaf teacher. By the time pure oralism was at its height, the number of deaf teachers had shrunk from 40% to only 14% of the total deaf education work force (Gannon, 1981, p.3). This viable career option for deaf adults was removed, leaving them to search for less desirable work.

In enforcing the oralist teaching framework, children were subjected to sitting on their hands, having their hands tied behind their backs, and receiving other hideous forms of punishment to deter them from signing. Even now, our older deaf population remembers vividly the variety of punishments enacted for breaking the stringent rules of oralism.

While Alexander Graham Bell channeled his great wealth and energy to establishing oral schools for deaf children (Arnold, 1984), Edward Miner Gallaudet continued his family's strong commitment to sign language. The lines were drawn, and the beginnings of a century-long battle for the soul of deaf education raged—often at the expense of the students served (Gannon, 1981).

Even though Deaf Americans lacked the power to force schools to halt the suppression of their language, they stubbornly persisted in using signs in their private lives and keeping their culture alive. A few vigorous advocates for signing kept the flame lit through the darkest days, insisting that the endless hours of speech training were leaving deaf students devoid of knowledge. The deaf community organized itself and attempted to change policy at local and state levels, though it experienced little success. Its most vocal members were the deaf students themselves, who had grown up under the oral system, and found it woefully lacking. It wasn't until the 1960s that sign language began to surface again in the education of deaf children.

The pendulum swing toward oralism also brought with it a movement of deaf students from residential schools to day schools and integrated classroom settings. The roots of this movement seem to have begun in Bell's strong conviction that deaf people should not associate with each other, for fear that this association would encourage deaf marriages and the continuation of deaf culture. Though vehemently opposed by most deaf people, many other people, including doctors, hearing parents, and their professional organizations, once again led the charge for a forced assimilation of the deaf student population. Perhaps the most serious threat came in the form of a seemingly well-meaning initiative, the Education for All

Handicapped Children Act of 1975 (Van Cleve & Crouch, 1989). This law mandated that all children should receive a "free, appropriate public education" in the "least restrictive environment." Many parents of disabled children welcomed the opportunity to have their children live at home and to enroll them in public schools. Regardless of its good intentions, the law strikes at the heart of the residential schools, where generations of deaf students have found their community, their language, and a shared culture. A related by-product of this law has been a shifting away of funds from the residential schools and shrinking enrollments. For some residential schools, it has meant a slow death, the painful closing of an institution that is dearly loved and valued.

Today, many deaf community members believe that "the dark world of oralism," in which educators tried to eliminate signing, has given way to an uncertain world of inclusion, where deaf children face "a different kind of isolation" (Padden & Humphries, 1988, p. 116). The deaf community's insistence on its status as a unique and culturally viable minority group seems at odds with the educational system of assimilation. A language-rich learning environment, where deaf students have full access to direct communication with everyone in their environment, is not even remotely possible in most current integrated settings. Given this situation, what can be done to ensure that deaf students have full access to the educational system? Are the cultural elements of the residential schools able to be adapted to the inclusion setting? What is a communicative, rich learning environment for deaf students, and how can one be nurtured and maintained? Is the essence of hearing/deaf peer relationships anemic in comparison to deaf/deaf relationships, or do they provide sufficient foundations on which to build solid friendships? How do the issues of isolation and alienation impact student learning? As we explore the answers to these questions, it is imperative that we listen to the stories of deaf students and the professionals who serve them. It is through their eyes that we can truly understand the complexity of issues that frustrate those children we serve.

Cultural Competency: Salient Values of the Deaf Community

Imagine—deafness not as a defect, but as a source of connection!
Imagine yourself deaf, growing up with a beautiful language,

visual literature, humor, and theater. Imagine taking pride in your identity
without any desire to become a member of the majority culture
(Halpern, 1996).

The critical juncture of communication and relationship building is culture. Many agree that educators can best serve deaf children by understanding the salient features of deaf culture in order to create culturally
competent learning environments for deaf students (Lane, 1992; Sass-Lehrer
et al., 1997; Seigel, 2001). While it certainly seems true that a rudimentary
understanding of the cultural heritage of deaf students would give educators greater insight into the world of being deaf, this knowledge should be
coupled with inquiry into the level of ownership that deaf students hold
to this heritage.

The salient values of deaf culture are tied to language, and the sites of
cultural transmission, namely residential schools. In the deaf community,
initial conversations usually begin by asking where you are from. A deaf
person often responds by naming the residential school attended, rather
than their hometown. Due to the fact that the majority of hearing parents do not learn to sign, depriving their child of meaningful family relationships, deaf friendships become extremely important to deaf people.
Friendships from their residential school days often last a lifetime.

For deaf people, sign language is often an "embodiment of their personal and cultural identity" (Sacks, 1989, p. 125). As with other languages, signed conversations have a certain etiquette that serves as both
an exclusive and inclusive gate into the culture and community of Deaf
people. For new signers, this etiquette, or lack thereof, gives the person
away (Brueggemann, 1995). But as Edward Miner Gallaudet, himself
wrote, the greatest value of sign language to the deaf is to be found in
"the facility it affords for free and unconstrained social intercourse"—
which in fullness of expression is in "no respect inferior, and is in many
respects superior, to articulated speech as a means of communicating
ideas" (Gallaudet, 1992).

"Speech and hearing thinking is negatively valued in deaf culture,"
while mastery of ASL and ASL storytelling are highly valued (Lane, 1992).
It is sometimes assumed that ASL does not have literature, since it is
not written down. However, there is a wealth of ASL literature—stories

woven around themes of how deaf people see their own lives, their world within the deaf community, and the outside world, namely, the hearing community (Humphries et al., 1994). Deaf literature often surfaces and flourishes at deaf events and informal gatherings—including vibrant ASL jokes, naming rituals, sign play, plays, fables, tall tales, stories, historical accounts, legends, anecdotes, poetry, and much more (Lane, 1992). Much of the literature of deaf culture is related directly, or indirectly to issues of power, control and domination between the hearing and deaf world.

In "My Third Eye," an original play created and performed by the National Theatre of the Deaf (1973), a brutal scene depicts a cast member's memories of watching a classmate being punished by dunking and caning—methods that were not unusual in oral schools (Padden & Humphries, 1988). The scene opens with a young woman being held tightly by two ominous figures. When she is asked to reproduce a word, she tries, but is unsuccessful in her attempt. Her head is forcefully dunked in an unseen bowl of water, as she squirms and tries to escape. Again and again she is instructed to speak clearly, but with each unsuccessful attempt she is repeatedly dunked. The scene ends with the young woman weak and near death, helplessly unable to escape (Padden & Humphries, 1988).

Humor that is culturally specific for a group is more than just language; it is a matter of experience (Rutherford, 1983) Often, humorous stories evolve of deaf people triumphing over adverse conditions. One favorite joke told by Deaf people is as follows:

> A deaf couple checks into a motel. They retire early. In the middle of the night, the wife wakes her husband, complaining of a headache, and asks him to go to the car and get some aspirin from the glove compartment. Groggy with sleep, he struggles to get up, puts on his robe, and goes out of the room to his car. He finds the aspirin, and with the bottle in hand he turns toward the motel, but he cannot remember which room is his. After thinking for a moment, he returns to the car, places his hand on the horn, holds it down, and waits. Very quickly the motel rooms light up, all but one. It's his wife's room, of course. He locks up his car and heads toward the room without a light. (Humphries, 1994)

This joke represents a turnaround of the power hearing people often exert over Deaf people. Other sources of humor center on the deaf experience—such as innovative ways to wake up a deaf person and poking fun at a hearing person's way of life.

Members of the deaf community highly value their deaf identity, as well as the collective value of deaf children. The shared experience of deafness generally overrides other dividing factors such as socioeconomic status or ethnicity. Fierce loyalty, hugs, and long goodbyes, are common markers of deaf culture, as is intermarriage. As many as 9 out of 10 deaf people marry other deaf in America (Lane, 1992). Deaf adults feel strongly about the need for deaf role models in the lives of deaf children and go out of their way to nurture these children with exposure to aspects of their culture. Deaf children who have had no exposure to deaf adults sometimes believe that they will grow up hearing, because they have never met a deaf adult. Many stories in deaf literature expand on this experience and serve as subtle reminders for the deaf adult population to be active in the lives of young deaf children. These cultural values that drive the deaf community are passed on from generation to generation as deaf children become deaf adults.

Cochlear Implants

For centuries, people believed that only a miracle could fully restore hearing to the deaf, but almost 50 years ago, scientists began to discover ways to electronically stimulate the auditory nerve (Loizou, 1998). Since then, teams of scientists from various disciplines including bioengineering, physiology, otolaryngology, speech science, and signal processing have contributed to the invention of the cochlear implant, a small electronic device that provides a sense of sound to many formerly deaf children and adults. According to the Food and Drug Administration's 2002 data, over 59,000 individuals worldwide have received implants; in the United States, 10,000 children have received implants, and nearly 13,000 adults have received them.

The implant consists of three parts: the *receiver*, implanted under the skin behind the ear with a wire that threads through the cochlea in the inner ear; a *headpiece*, a small magnetic disk that is worn behind the ear and consists of a microphone and transmitter; and the *speech processor*, often worn over the ear like a hearing aid. The cochlear implant, therefore, does not interpret sound, or even provide full access to speech; instead, it converts sound into electrical signals, sending these signals to the auditory nerve and then on to the brain. The results are a wildly variable set of outcomes.

While some children may demonstrate an understanding of complex running speech, other implanted children may gain only a basic awareness of sound. However, research does show that children implanted before the age of three have a far greater rate of success (Nussbaum, 2003), especially those engaged in a substantial training program for speech and lip reading. However, the results do not clearly identify the extent of influence from other factors, such as the motivation of the family, the socioeconomic status of implanted families or the involvement of a team. The long-term outcomes of this technology are still mostly unknown, due to the changing characteristics of both the cochlear implants themselves and the children who are receiving them (Nussbaum, 2003).

Since students with cochlear implants are involved in a highly individualized gradual process of understanding auditory input, educating students with cochlear implants provides educators with a unique challenge. The 1995 Annual Survey provided some insight into what trends are evident in implanted students. At that time, 58% of the students with implants reported using sign and speech to communicate, indicating that the majority of students with implants are still using both visual and auditory capacities for communication. The dependence on visual communication is an indicator that many students with cochlear implants are not yet ready to be fully educated in an exclusively auditory environment—indeed, they may never reach a level of auditory discrimination that would make this an appropriate placement. While parents often choose to place their implanted children in settings that offer the greatest opportunity to facilitate spoken language development, it is crucial that the placement also be evaluated related to promoting positive social opportunities (Nussbaum, 2003). Like all children, children with cochlear implants need to enjoy a learning environment where they feel comfortable communicating with their peers so that they can develop age-appropriate social skills, friendships, and behavior (Bat-Chava & Deignan, 2001). Therefore, even after implementation, parents should choose an educational placement for their child that focuses on the whole child and not just the development of speech and listening skills to the exclusion of content knowledge.

To many parents, the cochlear implant serves as a pathway for providing their deaf child with access to the family's relationships, culture, and language. Certainly, many hearing families are attracted to the notion of their special needs child becoming "normal." According to one cochlear implant corporation, one in five implanted deaf children learns to speak and can function successfully in the hearing world. Project Hope's 2000 Policy Brief states that children with at least two years of cochlear implant experience are placed in mainstream classrooms at twice the rate of deaf children without implants. Successfully implanted children therefore may be more able to attend their local schools with siblings, as well as to participate in community activities. These and other considerations make cochlear implants an attractive choice for many parents of deaf children.

3

Accountability and Legal
Influences in Deaf Education

THE PATH TOWARD INCLUSION BEGAN with the passage of the
Education for All Handicapped Children Act in 1975 (PL 94–142), now
known as the Individuals with Disabilities Education Act (IDEA). In one
sweeping act, Congress declared that the injustices that had plagued the
education of students with special needs would no longer be tolerated.
Built upon the social forces of the civil rights movement, Congress created
a strong foundation for the belief that all citizens could be educated and
that society, in the form of public education agencies, was responsible for
doing so (Ramsey, 1994). A bonding of the American vision of equality
and freedom, coupled with the influence of *Brown v. Board of Education*,
sent increasing numbers of children with disabilities into integrated environments under the belief that "separate cannot be equal."

The dominant message of IDEA is that all children, including children with disabilities, are entitled to a "free appropriate public education"
(FAPE) in the "least restrictive environment" (LRE). The "least restrictive environment" is not a place but a continuum of services requiring
high sensitivity to the individual needs of students (Rafferty, Piscitelli, &
Boettcher, 2003). This continuum includes options for encouraging social
interaction between students with disabilities and their nondisabled, age-
appropriate peers (Cohen, 1994a). Even though the law clearly requires
that all placement decisions be made on an individual basis through the
individual education plan (IEP), many parents and administrators have
interpreted LRE to mean placement within a public school. Clearly, in
some cases, this has led to an overshadowing of "appropriate" by the terminology of "least restrictive."

Prior to the passage of IDEA, millions of children received inadequate
education or were denied an education altogether. This piece of legislation
represented a conceptual starting point of a new attempt at addressing the
needs of all students (Siegel, 2000). Parents who had negative attitudes

toward separate educational placements seized the opportunity to enroll their children in the mainstream of the public schools. This movement paralleled a general trend in the U.S. of deinstitutionalization, normalization, and integration into the larger society.

As it became more apparent that a culture of inclusion was driving the understanding of LRE to mean a regular classroom, some policy makers became aware of the need to readdress this issue, especially for deaf children. In a special report, the Secretary of Education expressed concern that the "unique communication and related needs" of deaf children were being overlooked.

> The disability of deafness often results in significant and unique educational needs for the individual child . . . Compounding the manifest educational considerations, the communication nature of the disability is inherently isolating, with considerable effect on the interaction with peers and teachers that make up the educational process. This interaction, for the purpose of transmitting knowledge and developing the child's self-esteem and identity, is dependent upon direct communication. Yet communication is the area most hampered between a deaf child and his or her hearing peers and teachers. Even the availability of interpreter services in the educational setting may not address deaf children's needs for direct and meaningful communication with peers and teachers . . .
>
> [In light of this belief] the Secretary believes it is important that State and local education agencies, in developing an IEP for a child who is deaf, take into consideration:
>
> 1. Communication needs and the child's and family's preferred mode of communication;
> 2. Linguistic needs;
> 3. Severity of hearing loss and potential for using residual hearing;
> 4. Academic level; and
> 5. Social, emotional, and cultural needs including opportunities for peer interaction and communication.
>
> Any setting which does not meet the communication and related needs of a child who is deaf, and therefore does not allow for the provision of FAPE, cannot be considered the LRE for that child. (U.S. Department of Education, 1992)

Unfortunately, the belief that the regular classroom constituted the LRE had already become deeply embedded in the culture of schools, and the report was largely ignored. Even worse, local and state educational agencies now tend to make fiscal and programmatic decisions based on a belief that non-regular classrooms are disfavored (Siegel, 2001). In the end, there is *no* legal mandate for inclusion. Instead, policy supports the concept of the LRE as a continuum of placements, and the need for communicative rich environments as a basis for placement decisions. However, it is the *gap* between policy and practice that creates the misapplication of LRE for deaf and hard of hearing children—a misapplication that is real and prevalent.

Shared Responsibility for Deaf Students

Who holds the responsibility for achieving success with deaf students? Is it possible for a school, even one noted for academic achievement, to miss the calling to embrace all children? Do we discreetly value some children more than others? The No Child Left Behind Act (2001) clearly reminds us that excellence is expected for all children, including students with disabilities and those who do not look like their peers. Today our schools provide excellence for the top 20% of students, mediocrity for the next 40%, and they fail miserably the lowest-achieving 40% (Denbo, Grant, & Jackson, 2001), including many of those serviced by special education. To redress this goal of excellence for all students, school leaders and teachers must look within their own walls to the facets of diversity and evaluate honestly their ability to achieve excellence for all students.

The statistics on students served by special education are alarming. Only 50% of students who receive special education services graduate with standard diplomas, and 31% of students who have IEPs drop out of school before reaching graduation. Three to five years after leaving high school, close to half of those students are still unemployed (OSERS 23rd Annual Report to Congress on the IDEA, 2002). Deaf students do not fare much better. An estimated 50% of deaf students entering high school graduate without meeting the academic requirements for a diploma, leaving with a certificate instead. The dropout rate is also high, with 23% of residential school students dropping out during high school and an even higher 37% of deaf students in integrated schools dropping out before graduation. But the highest percentage is found in deaf students placed in day programs—deaf classes located within regular education schools—apart from both hearing peers and the deaf community, where the dropout rate almost doubles to 54% (Lane, Hoffmeister, and Bahan, 2002).

Where does the responsibility lie in reforming our efforts to reach these students? We must stop thinking and acting in isolated ways. Though special educators carry a certain responsibility for the implementation of services, it is imperative that regular education school leaders, teachers, and other staff members commit to the success of those students as well. In a recent national needs assessment, the top research and training need identified was educating administrators about appropriate services for students who are deaf or hard of hearing. This is not surprising, knowing that most of the administrators responsible for deaf education programs in public schools have limited experience or training in this area (Luckner et al., 2005).

Though the upward trend now shows that the majority of students receiving special education are being served in regular school buildings (2003), they often are left to struggle in a world of inclusion. Yet accountability measures force educators to look closely at the factors that affect the student achievement of these students and to evaluate their ability to promote their academic success.

But how is the national push for accountability influencing the education of deaf students? While state-specific data reporting procedures are required, it is exceedingly difficult to access the specific data of deaf students from their various education settings. While many programs do not have enough deaf students to constitute a subgroup for federal adequate yearly progress (AYP) considerations, state schools for the deaf may struggle to meet accountability requirements while assessing deaf students through a state test that seems inappropriate for their students.

Special Education Laws & Amendments

Influencing Deaf Education

P. L. 89–10, THE ELEMENTARY AND SECONDARY EDUCATION ACT OF 1965 (ESEA)

The Elementary and Secondary Education Act of 1965 became the statutory basis upon which early special education legislation was drafted. The amendment authorized grants to state institutions and state-operated schools devoted to the education of children with disabilities. This was the first federal grant program specifically targeting children and youth with disabilities. Another amendment in 1966 authorized grants for the education of students with disabilities at the local school level.

P. L. 93–280, THE EDUCATION AMENDMENTS OF 1974

The Education Amendments included Title VI, which was the Education of the Handicapped Act Amendments of 1974; an appropriate education for all children with disabilities was mentioned for the first time. It also gave parents the right to examine records kept in the student's file.

P. L. 94–142, THE EDUCATION FOR ALL HANDICAPPED CHILDREN ACT OF 1975

The Education for All Handicapped Children Act mandated a free, appropriate public education for all children with disabilities, ensured due process rights, mandated IEP's and LRE, and became the core of federal funding for special education. Though this law was passed in 1975, it did not go into effect until 1977.

P. L. 98–199, EDUCATION OF THE HANDICAPPED ACT AMENDMENTS OF 1983

The Education of the Handicapped Act Amendments of 1983 established services to support school-to-work transition and parent training and information centers. It also promoted early intervention and early childhood special education.

P. L. 99–457, EDUCATION OF THE HANDICAPPED ACT AMENDMENTS OF 1986

The Education of the Handicapped Act Amendments of 1986 mandated services for preschoolers and promoted state wide systems of early identification.

P. L. 101–476, EDUCATION OF THE HANDICAPPED ACT AMENDMENTS OF 1990

The Education of the Handicapped Act Amendments of 1990 renamed the law the Individuals with Disabilities Education Act (IDEA). It strengthened the law by mandating transition services and defining assistive technology.

P. L. 105–17, THE INDIVIDUALS WITH DISABILITIES EDUCATION ACT AMENDMENTS OF 1997

The Individuals with Disabilities Education Act Amendments of 1997 strengthen the role of parents, ensure access to the general curriculum, promote a focus on teaching and learning, and assist educational agencies in the cost of providing special education services.

Above information was accessed from the National Dissemination Center for Children with Disabilities. (The History of the IDEA, 1998)

P. L. 107–110, THE NO CHILD LEFT BEHIND ACT OF 2001

The No Child Left Behind Act of 2001 is current law. It strives to close the achievement gap with accountability, flexibility and choice. NCLB strengthens the accountability of the nation's schools through mandatory state assessments and by requiring schools to meet adequate yearly process goals. This accountability framework includes assessment, standards-based curriculum, teacher quality, and added resources for students in schools that do not meet annual benchmarks.

Above information was accessed from the U.S. Department of Education Web site (No Child Left Behind Law).

P. L. 108–446, THE INDIVIDUALS WITH DISABILITIES EDUCATION IMPROVEMENT ACT OF 2004

The reauthorized IDEA calls for special education reform based on paperwork reduction, early intervention, parental choice, and academic results for students—placing a renewed emphasis on ensuring children with disabilities are learning. It strives to improve educational results for students with disabilities by:
- making special education stronger for students and parents
- ensuring school safety and reasonable discipline
- reducing unnecessary lawsuits and litigation
- supporting teachers and schools
- reforming special education funding

U.S. Department of Education. (The Individuals with Disabilities Education Improvement Act of 2004—Bill Summary)

4 Confronting the Realities of Inclusion

INCLUSION—the idea that *all* children should and can learn in a regular classroom—has taken firm root in many school systems, even though it is not specifically required by law (Cromwell, 1997). Opposing inclusion would seem to advocate exclusion, even though some observers maintain that inclusion isn't always the best way to meet student needs. In their view, trying to force all students into the inclusion mold is "just as coercive and discriminatory as trying to force all students into the mold of a special education class or residential institution" (Kauffman, 1995). Some voices in the discourse of inclusion have even wondered whether, in the zeal to promote inclusion, some inclusionists have forgotten about the child (Block, 1999).

Though most educators would agree that some students do benefit from inclusive education, the question remains: Are there some children for whom "inclusion" is inappropriate? In the wake of No Child Left Behind, educators can no longer ask themselves if deaf students *can* learn in inclusive settings, but instead, can deaf students achieve *academic excellence* in inclusive settings? This analysis would not only support the underlying belief system that *all* children can learn but that all children have the right of reaching their own full individual potential of learning. Schools that expect less, or that are only capable of less, fail their students and the communities that support them (Denbo et al., 2001).

Serious questions have been raised about the ability of inclusive settings to foster adequate communicative learning environments for deaf students. It is apparent that many professionals are concerned with deaf children's lack of access to direct communication in inclusive settings (Siegel, 2001; Nowell, 1997; Ramsey, 1997; Schildroth, 1997, p. 10; Cohen, 1994, p. 7; Leigh, 1994; Stone, 1994; Winston, 1998; Stinson & Lang, 1994; Lane, 1992; Padden & Humphries, 1988; etc). The effects of communication deprivation can have deeply profound effects on the long-term welfare of the deaf child, resulting in diminished relationship building (Krever, 2002) and diminished linguistic latitude in vocabulary and conceptualization (National Center on Deafness, 2003).

In order for deaf and hard of hearing children to succeed in regular education placements, schools must be able to effectively integrate them into the social milieu and the learning activities of the school and classroom (Stinson and Lang, 1994). Yet the only way for deaf students to gain full access to the communication in the classrooms would be if the teachers and classmates were to become fluent in American Sign Language and use it in all communicative acts. Separate from this, significant communication barriers can greatly hinder the education of deaf students.

Deaf and hard of hearing students are among the ranks of students with special needs being placed in regular education classrooms. About 64% of these students receive some or all of their education in regular classrooms. Even though deaf students are placed within the category of "students with disabilities" or "special education students," their situation is unique in that 50% use sign language as their primary means of communication (Gallaudet Research Institute, 2005). Their use of a language apart from the majority language places them more realistically in the category of bilingual students. Deaf students' normal range of cognitive abilities also would be consistent with this placement. Many come from English-speaking families, unlike other bilingual children. In fact, research shows that more than 70% of these children do not share a language with their own parents and siblings (Gallaudet Research Institute, 2005). Instead, they share a language with a group of people with whom their families have very little contact.

The President's Commission on Excellence in Special Education (2002) embraces the notion of providing for and planning for the intellectual, social, and emotional development of the student receiving special education services. While there has been a focus on the placement of students in inclusive settings, there has been little concern for what happens to the child in the hallway, lunchroom, or after-school activities (Kluwin & Stinson, 1993). This framework of support is often lacking in our fervor to place children in inclusive settings (Banks, 1994). Without this framework, inclusion means "fear, confusion, neglect, and fragmentation" (p. 193).

An essential element of the support framework for building relationships is knowledge and respect for the cultures represented. Children who are competent members of their own culture seem to have a stronger sense of personal identity and of in-group membership; therefore, the role of educators is critical in helping students become confident members of their own culture (Shaw & Jamieson, 1995). People with disabilities have forged a group identity, sharing a common history of oppression and a common bond of resilience (S. E. Brown, 1996). Deaf students have a special set of culturally related issues. In order to understand deaf students, and their common identity, one must first recognize the two common ways of viewing deafness. The handicapped perspective views deaf people with pity, focusing on their inabilities instead of their abilities. The cultural perspective views deaf people as belonging to a culture equal with all the other cultures of the world and using a fully developed language—a perspective that views deaf people in a positive light, focusing on their potential and abilities (Wixtrom, 1992). An understanding of the cultural view of deafness will help the relationship-building partner to see the deaf person as an equal—a critical step in building trust. Schools that understand the deaf cultural perspective foster the belief that deaf students are equal to hearing students and can equally succeed.

Academic Achievement of Deaf Students

Regardless of category placement, deaf students' academic achievement has historically been low. The Stanford Achievement Test, 9th Edition (Harcourt Educational Measurement, 1996), showed 17–18-year-old deaf high school graduates scored fairly consistently on the fourth grade reading level (Holt, Traxler, & Allen, 1997). This same report indicates that only 3% of deaf high school seniors are reading at the same level as their hearing peers. Similar research on deaf education provided the impetus for the formation of the National Agenda (NA)—a coalition of parents, consumers, advocacy organizations, and educators who organized to improve educational opportunities for deaf and hard of hearing children. The NA leads the movement for reform in deaf education; their goal is that deaf children "leave school with the skills necessary to be productive adults" (*Press Release: National Agenda*, 2003).

Many attribute the lack in academic achievement to a system that does not provide quality, communication-based educational programs for deaf and hard of hearing children (Johnson, Liddel, & Erting, 1989; Siegel, 2001). The NA, also, does not see the problem as one of individual educators, but rather as a "larger systemic failure." It views the existing system as one that "does not understand the central role that communication plays for our children and how educational and personal growth requires an effective and age-appropriate communication mode and language" (*Press Release: National Agenda*, 2003). Sometimes in the past, standards were simply lowered when students didn't meet them; the reasons for failure were not addressed (Hanson, 2003; Johnson et al., 1989). In most cases, the monumental task of bringing a staff to competency in the language of deaf students has been a deterrent to all but a few residential schools for the deaf. Many adults working with deaf students are learning sign language as a second language later in life. Therefore, they may feel insecure and inept in communicating clearly in the child's first language. This fear of being misunderstood results in "linguistic overprotection," meaning the adult will "talk down" to or lessen the linguistic and cognitive complexity of their communication with the deaf child (Marschark & Spencer, 2003). Even so, it is becoming more apparent that rich communicative environments are necessary to help deaf students learn.

One indicator of successful social integration and communication access is the degree to which deaf students participate in classroom learning. While full access would seem to indicate the ability to participate in learning activities on an equal basis with hearing peers, in practice, such access rarely occurs (Stinson & Lang, 1994).

What are the barriers that deaf students experience in participating in the classroom? The first barrier is *lag time* between the spoken message and the interpreted message, which prevents the deaf student from equal participation. The lag time often leaves the student unable to respond or in danger of responding inappropriately, embarrassing themselves and others. The second barrier is the *rapid rate of discussion* or presentation that occurs when many speakers are involved in a lively discussion. As speakers jump in and out of a discussion very quickly, the message that comes through the interpreter is one long, undifferentiated string of words, without the visual breaking of looking from speaker to speaker. The third barrier to participation is *space*. Deaf students need to sit in areas of the classroom that maximize the range of their visual field; they must be able to see the instructor, the blackboard, and the interpreter all at once. This arrangement is highly dependent, though, on the cooperation of the teacher, interpreter, and seating arrangement. As the teacher moves around the room, an extra challenge is created as the deaf student attempts to watch the teacher for expression and body language cues and the interpreter for content. The final barrier to participation is *language*. Though the obvious result of not sharing a language is confusion, the barrier of language also prevents deaf students from participating in class relationship building. The lighthearted joking or teasing that may create a warm and comfortable learning environment for hearing students may be confusing to deaf students. Very often people laugh at jokes that are funny in English but are not funny in ASL. The jokes either are heavily dependent on English, or they rely on a particular tone of voice to be conveyed. ·

Full participation includes involvement in activities outside of class such as eating lunch with friends and visiting a friend's house (Stinson & Whitmore, 1992b). In these situations that deaf students tend to segregate or feel alienated if no deaf peer group exists, which suggests that social mainstreaming may be more difficult to achieve than academic mainstreaming (Foster, 1988).

Not all deaf and hard of hearing students meet failure in integrated educational learning environments. In fact, some students are highly successful in integrated settings. Interviews with 20 successful students who were receiving most of their education in regular classrooms, as well as from their parents and other professionals, revealed some very interesting commonalities:

- All deaf students were fully involved in athletics or other extracurricular activities.
- All students were characterized as being outgoing and with high self-esteem.
- All students came from very supportive families.
- All students were described as having good social skills—easily making friends and teaching them sign language.

- All students demonstrated a strong inner drive, combined with high expectations for themselves.
- All students had a good reading level.
- Finally, all students had a strong desire to be independent and demonstrated good self-advocacy skills. (Luckner and Muir, 2001)

Other positive factors noted in the study included effective teachers and interpreters, collaboration of early intervention providers, and collaboration among the student's educational team (Luckner & Muir, 2001).

While the similarities among successful students are striking, only a small percentage of deaf students share all of these characteristics. Therefore, as more and more deaf students are being placed in integrated settings, it is vital that the characteristics needed for success both academically and socially be recognized and encouraged to the greatest extent possible.

Language Learning Environments

Access to communication remains the greatest concern in placing deaf children in public schools. Many of these children do not receive sufficient reciprocal interaction from teachers and peers to develop normal language and social skills. Hearing children have hundreds of conversational exchanges each day, but what about deaf children? One case study is particularly illustrative of the deaf child's predicament. Jamieson (1995) observed a deaf boy in a fully integrated third-grade classroom. The boy was the only signing student in not only the school but the district. During the school day, this student interacted primarily with adults in his environment. On the playground, interaction with peers was basically categorized as directives, or what Ramsey (1997) has labeled, "caretaker talk." Almost all interaction both in the classroom and outside the classroom was initiated by others and did not lead to more than one turn exchange. When the deaf student initiated an interaction, the hearing students ignored 10%–20% of these initiations.

The teacher also communicated with the boy using more directives and closed questions than she used with other students. This technique led the deaf student to provide one-word or one-gesture responses, in contrast to the higher-level thinking skills the teacher encouraged from the hearing students. Both the deaf education teacher and the interpreter showed this same tendency to use directives or closed question forms with the deaf student during tutorials (Jamieson, 1995).

The interpreter contributed to the student's restricted access to language by failing to interpret significant communication during transitions and while the teacher was instructing others in the classroom. The interpreter did not interpret other students' comments, so the deaf child never "heard" the other children's thinking. While other students were working independently, the interpreter tended to over-support the deaf student, giving him very little opportunity to work independently or to ask the teacher for help. These and other findings lead us to an even greater concern for deaf students' ability to access language in inclusive settings. Educators must realize that effective shared communication is critical for facilitating language development, and therefore careful thought should be given to the linguistic, social, and intellectual development of deaf children (Marschark, Lang, & Albertini, 2002).

Relationship Building for Deaf Students in Inclusive Settings

A substantial body of research supports the notion that social variables are integral rather than incidental to learning (Ragizzino, Resnik, Utne-O'Brien, & Weissberg, 2003). Successful children are likely to be active and socially involved with their peers and teachers (Chen, Rubin, & Li, 1997; Feshbach & Feshbach, 1987). They communicate ideas effectively; listen to, evaluate, and integrate the ideas of others; elicit ideas and input from others; and ask teachers and peers for help when necessary (Ragizzino et al., 2003). Successful students tend to build relationships within the school body and in turn develop a deep sense of belonging (Osterman, 2000). This sense of belonging leads to a feeling of " membership," of being an integral part of the classroom and school community (Antia & Stinson, 2002). Membership can be contrasted with "visitorship"—a feeling that the deaf students are visitors and don't really belong in the class. When programs treat deaf students as visitors, they compound the barriers that deaf students face in obtaining a quality education with hearing students, especially in relationship building.

Concerns relating to relationship building and alienation are common themes in the discourse related to the integration of deaf students. A child is not being included if he simply sits beside his classmates but does not interact with them or comprehend what the teacher is saying (Ross, 1978). This seemingly impenetrable barrier can hinder the relationships normally found within the school walls.

The barrier of communication between the deaf and hearing worlds is not easily overcome by gesturing and writing notes. Many deaf students are left with the option of teaching their peers sign language in an effort to create their own peer group. Though a small percentage of hearing students may learn the manual alphabet, or a few signs, hearing peers rarely learn to communicate at a conversational level.

Despite these barriers, though, some deaf high school students who have been in both mainstream and deaf schools are glad they attended mainstream schools in their early years because it allowed them to stay close to home. They also believe that the mainstream environment gave them an understanding of the hearing world and helped them develop skills to communicate in both deaf and hearing environments. However, by early adolescence, most of these students come to the realization that something important is missing from their lives (Wilson, 1997). One deaf teenager said,

> I think I'm a good example of why it's very important to have a social life because without it you can't grow, you can't learn; because you can read all the books in the world, but they don't teach you about the world because you don't have a social life. You don't know who you are. You don't know how to interact with people. I mean, for example, I remember a big reason why I was so depressed. I felt trapped in my home, in my hearing high school. I felt like I went there for years and years, that starting from the seventh grade up to tenth grade I didn't change. I was the same person . . . It feels like you stay your age. You become smarter and smarter, but you won't develop like in a regular teenage way. You're stuck in time like a 13- or 14-year-old.

A common theme emerging from the comments of these deaf teenagers was an innate drive that pulled them toward each other so they could mature as teenagers. As they moved into a deaf learning environment, students described a socializing process that took place: "In classes, the students had the opportunity to learn new skills such as public speaking. Outside of class, they learned how to make and keep friends, how to say 'no,' and how to manage their time independently. In the comfort of being with other bright deaf teenagers, their confidence grew" (Wilson, 1997).

An earlier study corroborates this view of graduates of residential programs (Mertens, 1989). These young adults described their social experiences significantly more positively than did graduates of mainstream programs. Their reasons included teachers' ability to sign, opportunities to socialize with friends, and participation in after-school activities. But positive feelings in mainstream programs were also noted, such as availability of supportive services, ability to voice and lipread (for those that felt skilled in this area), parent involvement, and the opportunity to encourage deaf awareness in others (Mertens, 1989).

A more recent study by Sheridan (2001), noted that most of the deaf children interviewed conveyed strong positive perceptions of self. Although the children gave examples of situations where they felt uncomfortable or alienated, they did show positive ways of coping. This finding was not consistently evident in the interviews I conducted.

School: A Learning Community

Essentially, schools are networks of sustained relationships. The social exchanges that occur and the perceived meaning attributed to them are central to a school's functioning (Byrk & Schneider, 2002). As the movement toward social learning gains greater recognition among educators, many feel that schools should transform to a more personalized focus—a focus on the development of student-student and student-adult relationships (Hoffman & Levak, 2003) The collaboration needed at every level confirms the overriding consideration, which is that every person concerned with integrated education must want it to work well. "That attitude must be voiced by administrative leadership and it must permeate the professional staff" (Barton, 1977). A network of relationships is built to support the student, as well as individual relationships with the student.

Relationship building within a school also presents a clear reflection of the schools overall cultural competency. A school in which an ethic of care is evident fosters a sense of "community" and "family," with a focus on responsibilities and relationships instead of on rights and rules (Ferreira, Smith, & Bosworth, 2002). When students are asked to identify the elements of a caring school, they emphasize the importance of teacher-student relationships and student-student relationships, (Silver, 2003).

Educators have long realized the importance of developing caring relationships with students. This teacher-student relationship is vital because "students cannot be taught nor can learning be fostered until they are convinced the teacher cares about them" (Bulach, Brown, & Potter, 1998, p. 442). To open the relationship door, teachers need to know their students and to demonstrate a genuine interest in them (Mendes, 2003). The two behaviors most often used in fostering caring learning communities are "anxiety reducing behaviors" and a "willingness to listen" (Bulach, Brown, and Potter, 1998, p. 9). Teachers who act to reduce anxiety maintain eye contact, call students by name, and greet students as they enter the classroom. Interestingly, these anxiety-reducing measures involve minimal language and can easily be used by regular education teachers with deaf students. Demonstrating a willingness to listen is more difficult for the regular education teacher because it is heavily dependent on a shared language and may be supported or distorted by the intrusion of a third-party interpreter.

Student-teacher interactions are also important means of clarifying and resolving conflict in social expectations (Schloss, Selinger, Goldsmith, & Morrow, 1983). In light of the apparent deficit in deaf students' social skills, this relationship is even more important. Its value may be further extended by the fact that a number of students are not able to fluently communicate with their own parents. Research indicates that deaf students prefer teachers who are warm, friendly, and caring (Lang et al., 1993, 1994). But in the inclusive classroom, the deaf student interacts with the teachers, peers, and curriculum through the interpreter. When others speak to the deaf child, the information is funneled through the interpreter. Though there is interpreted interaction, the effect of the intrusion of an interpreter on the building blocks of a relationship is not fully known. The lack of direct communication may significantly hinder the relationship building between deaf students and their teachers, peers, and others in the school building.

Peer Relationships

One of the ideals of inclusive education is to create opportunity for deaf and hearing children to develop friendships. The hope is that students educated side by side will find a method of communicating and a pathway toward friendship. But for many students, even in a crowded classroom, school can be the loneliest place of all (Osman, 1982; Stinson & Whitmire, 1992a).

Peer interaction—teaching children to share, to help, to comfort, and to empathize with others—plays an important part in child development (Benard, 1990). Peer interaction can also facilitate higher reasoning and critical thinking skills (Anderson & Soden, 2001). But the research on peer interaction between hearing and deaf students in integrated settings has been alarming. Despite well-meaning efforts to teach hearing students sign language, it still is rare for a hearing child to learn enough sign language to engage in a conversation with a deaf child (Schildroth & Hotto, 1997). Even when several deaf children are present in the classroom, the hearing children's signing is either completely incomprehensible and confusing to deaf children, or it is understandable to the deaf children but impoverished (Ramsey, 1997). Most interaction takes the form of directives or evaluation, and the hearing children tend to adopt a patronizing attitude toward deaf children. Signed conversations between hearing and deaf students are limited to the signs the hearing students know. Therefore, their conversations involve present events, directives, and closed questions, all of which lead to only one turn exchange and a minimal response. Although several hearing students may want to interact with deaf students, they quickly became overwhelmed with their inability to sign their message and, therefore, give up (Shaw and Jamieson, 1995).

Relationship building between deaf and hearing children is rare and takes a considerable amount of time. Though hearing students are able to adapt fairly quickly to new classrooms, teachers, and peers each year (or semester), deaf students can become easily frustrated at having to start over educating everyone in their environment (Saur et al., 1986). This frustration can be accentuated if the deaf student has previously worked hard to teach peers sign language. The slow process of creating your own peer group can be interrupted and devastated by the forced changing of classes. In light of this understanding, it may be helpful for schedules to be created by taking into account the preferred peer groups of deaf children.

For peer relationships to be constructive, they must create feelings of belonging and acceptance, rather than rejection and alienation (Stinson & Whitmire, 1992b). A study of the quality of friendships among deaf adolescents to that of hearing students found the hearing students reported higher friendship quality and lower levels of loneliness than the deaf adolescents (Krever, 2002). The findings support previous research that suggests deaf students are at risk in their peer relations (Anitia, 1982). Studies such as these have created a growing belief that the lack of effective communication with others, and a lack of appropriate social models, can impede social adjustment.

An interesting element of peer friendships, though, is the possible imbalance in the definition of a friend. A deaf student might believe another student is a "friend" just because they wave to each other every morning, while a hearing student may only attribute the title of friend to people who share the same views or values. Also, hearing peers may overestimate their own social acceptance of deaf students. Though most hearing students may claim that deaf students are well accepted in school, they also report that deaf students don't work as hard and would be better off in a special school (Cambra, 2002). Therefore, it seems hearing students recognize a gap in their social and academic experiences.

Deaf students may have more social success in school if they are successful athletes (i.e., heroes on the ball field). The gifted aptitude of athletes seems to somehow overshadow the difference, or even glorify it (Luckner & Muir, 2001; Osman, 1982; Stewart & Stinson, 1992). Though research has not yet clearly identified the perspectives of deaf athletes in integrated settings, it does seem that peers may more readily embrace these students.

Bullying and Oppression of Deaf Students

While some deaf students have reported a sense of being accepted by peers because "everyone thinks signing is cool," others have endured bullying and oppression (Kluwin & Stinson, 1993). Peers can make school life enjoyable or nearly intolerable for students in integrated settings. Since students' attitudes toward diversity may not be shared by the adults in the building, the peer subculture in public schools should be understood and monitored by school leaders and teachers (Boyd, 1992). Any benefit of inclusion can quickly be offset by the reality of social rejection, antipathy, and the overt cruelty of peers toward someone who is, or is perceived as, different (Saur et al., 1986).

Issues such as harassment, teasing, and bullying are issues far broader than disability. Exclusion is not always about difference, but rather it is about a student culture's response to difference (Sapon-Shevin, 2003). Both bullying and oppression represent a definite imbalance of power where there is no acknowledgement of human rights, nor a place for negotiation. Students who are exposed to negative actions have difficulty defending themselves (Olweus, 2003). Too often this behavior is unseen by teachers and school leaders and unreported by students. Students say they don't report these incidents to adults because they believe that either the adults will do nothing, or their actions will be ineffective (Cooper & Snell, 2003). Unfortunately, research shows the students are right (Cooper & Snell, 2003; Frey, 2002).

Bullying attitudes may possibly reflect the attitudes of the bully's parents or of school administrators who feel that special education students "don't belong." If the bully feels support in this perception, "then we have reason to be concerned about the resiliency, coping skills, and safety of the deaf and hard of hearing students in public school classrooms" (McCrone, 2004, p. 4). For some deaf students, bullying results in lifelong emotional damage and may result in attempts at suicide.

Bullying can even further socially isolate deaf students from their academic environment. As heartbreaking cases of oppression and bullying emerge concerning deaf students, we see an urgent need to promote school culture reform (Wells, 2002). Every day in our schools, children with disabilities are threatened, teased, taunted, and tormented. (*Preventing Bullying: A Manual for Schools and Communities*, 1998). "If U.S. citizens abroad were subjected to the violence that many of our students face daily, our government might well intervene with military force" (Denbo et al., 2001).

Feelings of Isolation

As humans, we all share the need to interact with others (Strong, Silver, Perini, & Tuculesco, 2003). But the lack of communication and quality relationships often lead deaf students to feelings of loneliness and isolation (Mertens, 1989; Stinson & Whitmire, 1992b). This finding is profound in light of our understanding that alienated students seem to have a diminished learning capacity (Weissberg, Resnik, Payton, & O'Brien, 2003).

The feeling of isolation may be exacerbated if a deaf child is alone in the educational setting, and more than 6,000 are (*Annual Survey of Deaf and Hard of Hearing Children and Youth*, 2003). Is it possible for schools to satisfy the needs of a single deaf student? The answer may revolve around what many authors have called the "critical mass theory." This theory states that a sufficient number of deaf classmates in school is needed in order to support the student-to-student and student-to-teacher interaction basic to the learning process, while fostering social and cultural cohesion among them.

Feelings of isolation may be even more intense for deaf students who have spent years working to improve their speech with speech therapists and teachers but later realize that they are still not capable of being understood. Students in integrated settings may come to this realization at a fairly young age because they are faced with frustrations in communication on a daily basis. Although high-profile school violence incidents in Colorado, Arkansas, Kentucky, Mississippi, and Virginia have focused the nation's attention on alienated students, alienated students rarely go on violent shooting sprees. Instead, students who feel they have no place in schools disengage psychologically, and often physically, from those schools. The result is lower achievement levels and higher dropout rates (D. Brown, 1999). When one student is not a full participant in his or her school community, then we all are at risk (Sapon-Shevin, 2003).

5   Educational Interpreting

A DEAF CHILD'S LANGUAGE DEVELOPMENT, social acceptance, and academic achievement is deeply and profoundly affected by one person—the educational interpreter. As more students move to integrated learning environments, more interpreters are needed to provide access to those learning environments. In fact, an estimated 60% of sign language interpreters work with the estimated 60% of deaf students who learn in mainstream settings (Burch, 2005). But despite the 25 years of mandated services in public schools, there has been little systematic inquiry into the location or the qualifications of the current work force of educational interpreters (Burch, 2002).

Because the interpreter is the channel for all communication and instruction, it is important to understand the quality of service of this middle person. Winston (1994a) emphasized that even though an interpreter may be able to provide a form of access, the education establishment does not adequately address the educational and communicative requirements of deaf children in classrooms by simply providing interpretation. Winston believes that before a rational discussion of interpreting can occur, three myths of interpreting must be exposed: (1) the myth that interpreting is a simple substitute for direct communication and teaching; (2) the myth that interpreted education is an "included" education, and (3) the myth that there is an adequate number of qualified interpreters to meet the needs of full inclusion.

Interpreting is often assumed to give deaf students equal access to the world of communication and education. But this widely held belief that the interpreter "signs exactly what the teacher says" is known as a fallacy among interpreters and interpreting theory (Winston, 1994a). No matter how skilled the teacher or student, the interpreter is still the one to process the communication, always affecting the message to some degree. The very process of taking in material presented in one language and then conveying it into another language makes the result *not* the same (Winston, 1994a).

Effective interpreters have the skills to interpret everything from algebra to biology to history. But how many educational interpreters are effective? Do they have specialized training in how to interpret within the school system? Do interpreters have a code of ethics that guides them to make good choices and not help students to cheat?

Obviously, there is a need for inquiry into the specific elements of educational interpreting. Some questions of importance are addressed within the body of the discourse in the field of educational interpreting, while other questions are left unanswered—representing a need for more research. Unfortunately, the areas that seem of greatest significance to the education of deaf children are those that reveal the most grave of situations.

Is There Available an Adequate Number of Highly Skilled Educational Interpreters to Meet the Needs of Deaf Students?

As the number of deaf and hard of hearing children placed in integrated settings has soared in recent years, so has a parallel increase in demand for educational interpreters (Burch, 2005; Yarger, 2001). Unfortunately, a severe shortage of qualified interpreters throughout the United States has been a clear concern in the literature (Dahl & Wilcox, 1990; Gustason, 1985; Hayes, 1992; Jones, Clark, & Soltz, 1997; Yarger, 2001).

Though the research on educational interpreting has been scant, it does seem that the answers are highly varied by location. While one interpreter may have graduated from a respected interpreter training program, another educational interpreter may simply have learned some signs from a book.

As more and more deaf and hard of hearing students are placed in local school districts, administrators are making decisions about hiring and assigning interpreters—often without knowing the role or the function of the interpreters, or their level of skills (Patrie, 1994). Faced with the difficulty of hiring and evaluating interpreters in a language they do not know, many have turned to the Educational Interpreter Performance Assessment (Schick & Williams), a tool now being used in 15 states to evaluate the skills of educational interpreters (Schick & Williams, 2003). Still, most interpreters report that their interpreting skills were not evaluated before they were hired (Jones, Clark, & Stoltz, 1997), nor have they been since (Yarger, 2001).

Without formal certification or degree requirements for educational interpreters, the variety of abilities is alarming. Jones, Clark, and Stoltz (1997) surveyed 222 educational interpreters in three states and found that many interpreters have been poorly trained and lack certification. This finding was reemphasized by Schick, Williams, and Bolster in 1999 when their study of 59 interpreters revealed that slightly less than half of the interpreters were not able to perform at a level considered minimally acceptable (Schick, Williams, & Bolster, 1999). These findings are highly disturbing because of the direct impact of interpreting effectiveness on the academic achievement of deaf students.

In rural areas, the lack of qualified interpreters may be even more extreme. Yarger (2001) examined the experiences, preparation, and perceptions of educational interpreters employed in rural areas; of the 63 respondents, only 10 had completed interpreter preparation programs, with 5 of those having no course work related to interpreting in an educational setting. None of the interpreters working in elementary or secondary school held any kind of certification. Of further concern was the lack of skill in the respondents. The EIPA was administered to each respondent, with a possible score of 0–5. A test score of 3.5 is considered "coherent," though this score would indicate multiple errors—a level so low that the deaf student would need to have extensive compensatory skills in order to comprehend the message being communicated. Sadly, the mean score on the EIPA for the educational interpreters tested was 2.6—markedly lower than even the "coherent" score. With this ominous discovery, Yarger suggests that schools should place interpreters who have the strongest abilities with students who have the fewest compensatory skills—specifically elementary and preschool children.

The scarcity of qualified interpreters, coupled with concern about the quality of interpretation, has been evident throughout the literature and points to a clear need for more specialized training. While some interpreters overestimate their skills, others quickly identify their own lack of ability in sign-to-English interpreting and receptive skills, insufficient vocabulary, and limited knowledge and understanding of ASL (Yarger, 2001). Winston (1994a) expressed concern that interpreters are not prepared to provide even minimally satisfactory interpreting for deaf students. This would seem to indicate a need for reform in interpreter training programs to include more specialized training courses in educational interpreting.

Dahl and Wilcox's study (1990) gathered information from interpreter training programs concerning the specialized training that graduates receive in educational interpreting issues. Their results suggest that graduates of interpreter training programs are only partially prepared to engage in employment as educational interpreters, desperately needing more training in educational interpreting issues.

Interpreter training programs, though, have long fought a battle of preparing students for interpreting in record time. Brian Cerney, an ASL interpreter trainer and author of *The Interpreting Handbook*, explains, "If I told you that I could make you a United Nations interpreter in two years—in a language completely unknown to you—would you believe me? And yet, that is the charge given to most two-year training programs." The cumbersome task of teaching an entire language, and then teaching how to interpret that language, leaves little time for specialized classes. Therefore, the task of learning how to best meet the needs of deaf and hard of hearing students is left up to the interpreters, as they struggle on their own in their new roles.

What Are the Realities of an Interpreted Learning Environment?

It is assumed that through interpreting, deaf children gain equal access to education. But many believe that no matter how skilled the interpreter, an interpreted education still is only a second-hand education (Winston, 1994b). Roach (2002) also maintains that the placement of a deaf student in a mainstream classroom with an interpreter is often done with little proactive thought. In reality, Roach claims that the formula looks more as follows:

Deaf student + inexperience with an interpreter and language delay
+ unskilled signer + "Helper" approach
+ regular education teacher + low expectations and ignorance
+ hearing students + pity and fear
= NEGATIVE OUTCOME (blamed on the deaf student's "disability") (p. 1)

In order to change this scenario to a more empowering learning environment for deaf students, it is important to analyze the purpose of the education interpreter (Roach, 2002).

Do Some Deaf Children Have the Same Interpreter for Years?

Interpreters are often hired with the expectation they will "follow" the student from preschool to high school (Yarger, 2001). When the interpreter is highly skilled across subjects, there may be some benefit to building a relationship with a student over an extended time period. However, if the interpreter is less skilled, the long-term assignment can severely hinder the student's academic achievement, causing irreparable damage for life.

Many interpreters are aware of the need for students to have multiple communication partners. In Yarger's study (Yarger, 2001), one interpreter explained, "I am the only one in his environment who understands 100% of what he signs." Another interpreter agreed: "I've been with her now [for 5 years]. I have often wondered how good that is for a child, and it bothers me that I have been her only interpreter" (p. 21).

How Does Interpreting Change the Message?

La Pointe (1997) writes, "To eliminate misconceptions, one must first separate sign language from the interpreting process" (p. 6). Interpreting is not just the act of changing one language to another, or from one mode to another; instead, it must take into account the intelligibility of the message (Kluwin & Stewart, 2001).

Research has not directly evaluated the intelligibility of the message in educational settings, but some authors have pointed to a clear difference between interpreted message and the teacher's intended message. One important factor to consider is if accurateness is evident between the original and the interpreted message. Eye contact, body posture, vocal intonation, and cultural expectations can each deeply affect the comprehension of deaf students (Cerney, 2004b). Even if the signs reflect the spoken message, the manner in which the message is given can greatly change the meaning of the message.

Even so, there is virtually no reliable, data-based information on whether young deaf children can receive the same educational benefits from using an interpreter as from direct instruction. But, even with this lack of data, there are good reasons to suspect that elementary and middle school students are less likely able to benefit from an interpreter than high school and college students (Schildroth & Hotto, 1997). For many, this may be due to the fact that they have not yet developed a first language.

What Kinds of Errors Can be Present in the Interpreting Process?

The interpreting process is a highly complex cognitive process and therefore requires a grounding in both the source language and the target language, as well as the interpreting process itself. Taylor (1993) identified 59 distinct measurable variables required for effective interpreting from English to ASL and an additional 41 variables for ASL to English (Taylor, 2002). All of these variables are required for accuracy in each act of educational interpreting.

Any part of the interpreted message that is not equivalent in meaning to the original message is considered an error (Taylor, 2002). Errors can be categorized by their frequency and severity. Low frequency errors may occur rarely, while high frequency errors occur repeatedly. Severity refers to the degree of inaccuracy, and the resulting miscomprehension that can occur.

Cokely (1992) recognized three specific types of errors: omissions, additions, and substitutions. Interpreter omissions happen when information is left out. For example, many novice interpreters only interpret what the teacher says. Therefore, the student sees the interpreter sign "Five plus five is . . . [pause] Right!" but they never see the answers. Novice interpreters also may not interpret information they themselves missed, instead of asking for clarification. So the students see the interpreter sign "Turn to page . . . [pause]," but they are not told the page number. Omissions are often considered severe errors, because the meaning is not retrievable by the audience (Taylor, 1993). Cokely recognizes the error of additions as another deviance from the source text. When the interpreter adds information to the source text, then the meaning can be changed drastically. A third error Cokely recognizes is the error of substitutions. When interpreters do not understand the source message, or perhaps do not agree with it, they may substitute their own message for the original one. All of these errors can expand or restrict the original meaning in the source text, or they can completely deviate from the original message. In Cokely's study, a high number of errors per interpreter was revealed—from 20 errors in 5 minutes, to 139 in 8 minutes of interpreting. Omissions represented the highest percentage of error type (up to 50%). This data is even more startling in that it is based on the performance of certified interpreters. Sadly, most educational interpreters are much less skilled and would likely produce a greater number of errors.

While an interpreter is interpreting the student's signs into spoken English, errors can also be present. Perhaps the most common errors are in additions or omissions, based on the interpreter's lack of understanding of the student. Another motivation for error may be that the interpreter wants the student to "look good," changing the message in order to match a perceived "more appropriate" response. Either way, the interpreter is misrepresenting the deaf student.

It is important to recognize that all interpreters make errors, but clearly, not all errors are equally serious for the student. Effective interpreters will recognize errors and attempt to correct them by asking for clarification or correcting themselves when needed. But errors that eliminate the student's ability to retrieve the original message may be the greatest detriment to student achievement. In Cokely's study, the interpreters were all certified, and 50% of these certified interpreters were also children of deaf parents. Nevertheless, their errors were recognizable. If well-trained certified interpreters are prone to errors, how much greater would be the errors of untrained, uncertified interpreters currently providing interpreting services to deaf students in classrooms.

By Having an Interpreter, Are Deaf Students Provided Full Access to Their Learning Environment?

Since it is not physically possible to interpret everything heard, interpreters must make value choices about which information to select as accessible to deaf students. The amount to which interpreters filter out some of the information presented varies. For example, the following communication acts may not be interpreted: sounds in the environment, group reaction vocalizations, parts of lively discussions—in which people interrupt each other or talk over each other, side comments, puns and plays on words, specialized vocabulary for which no sign exists, laughter, teacher feedback directed to other students, student-to-student comments, etc.

In Jamieson and Shaw's study (1995), the interpreter consistently failed to sign as the teacher verbally helped prepare the students for transition, such as, "You've just got a couple of minutes left." Therefore, the change from one activity to the next was abrupt for the deaf student, making him appear slower than the other students. Also, the teacher-class interaction continued for the hearing children when the teacher was not teaching the entire group, but circulating, commenting, and questioning the students. The hearing students were able to overhear this interaction, but it was not interpreted for the deaf student. This also gave no opportunity for the deaf student to "hear" the other children's thinking.

How Does Interpreting Affect the Relationship Building of Deaf Students?

An interpreted education means that every interaction includes three people, not two. It is not normal to have to include an adult when you ask someone for your first date; it is cumbersome to whisper to another classmate through an interpreter in school. Therefore, the "included" deaf student is actually "excluded" from *normal* interaction (Winston, 1994a).

In the classroom, the interpreter facilitates communication turns (Chafin Seal, 1998) and therefore exerts a certain control over the communica-tion process. Roy (1989, 1992) indicated that interpreters are the ones who mediate turns between deaf and hearing parties in a discussion. One frustration for many deaf students with inexperienced interpreters is that they rarely get a turn in the discussion. Many deaf students give up trying to take turns and become passive observers of the class rather than actively participating.

The extent that communicating through an interpreter hinders rela-tionship building for deaf students is deserving of further research. Social questions have been largely left unanswered: How does the student feel with an interpreter following them around all day? How does the inter-preter's presence affect interactions with classmates—gossip, jokes, and secrets? The answers can only come from the lived experiences of deaf students. In reading the interview responses of deaf students, you will find that their voices are integral to the focus of this book.

Some of the filtering out by the interpreter may fall into the category of relationship building. While the student is given access to the direct instruction of the teacher, he or she may miss communicative acts that foster the culture or climate of the school. This would be consistent with Shaw and Jamieson's later study (1997), which found that the discourse to which the student was exposed was primarily academic. In this study, they videotaped one deaf student for three hours in a regular education classroom. Interestingly, they reported that the deaf student interacted predominantly with the interpreter and also that the student received more direct instruction from the interpreter than from the teacher. In their earlier study, Shaw and Jamieson (1995) reported that the deaf student interacted only occasionally with the classroom teacher and that the interpreter initiated interactions with the deaf student almost three times more frequently than the classroom teacher.

Does the Deaf Child Build a Strong Relationship With the Interpreter?

The relationship between interpreter and student can become very strong, especially in cases of bonding over a long period of time or when the interpreter becomes the personal advocate for the student. These relationships can last a lifetime.

Interpreter-student relationships may be strengthened when injustice is realized by the interpreter. Harvey (2003) believes that although interpreters are expected to be neutral, this goal is psychologically unfeasible on an emotional level. Within the normal day-to-day exchanges of deaf children in hearing school, unintentional misunderstandings, and even purposeful acts of oppression, can occur. Interpreters may become empathetic toward the child and even feel worse because they are part of the communication process that is delivering the hurtful remarks. Empathy, alone, is an acceptable emotion, but it should not lead the interpreter to become overprotective of the student in order to shield him or her from pain.

Though little research has been conducted on interpreter-student relationships, they may in some ways parallel the relationship between some students with disabilities and their paraprofessionals. In the article *Working with Paraprofessionals* (Giangreco, 2003), the author posits that separating students with disabilities within the classroom isolates them from their peers and may encourage insular relationships between these students and the paraprofessionals assigned to them. Overdependence on paraprofessionals can adversely affect the social and academic growth of students, resulting in inadequate instruction and peer interactions (p. 52). Since many interpreters of deaf students are asked to perform the role of not only an interpreter but also a paraprofessional, it seems this concern would only be amplified. Based on Giangreco's examples, the following would be considered as problematic and unacceptable actions:

- An interpreter provides the student's primary literacy instruction.
- The student is removed from access to activities at the discretion of the interpreter.
- The student spends 80% or more of his or her time with an interpreter.
- The student spends the majority of his or her social time alone with an interpreter.
- The interpreter makes the majority of day-to-day curricular and instructional decision.

If these behaviors are unacceptable for paraprofessionals, it is also true that these should be considered unacceptable conditions for interpreters as well—and certainly not required of them. In light of these considerations, it is not surprising that many deaf children develop a strong relationship with their interpreters. Since research has not probed the unique relationship between the deaf child and the interpreter, the following interview responses provide focus in collecting baseline knowledge of this area.

6

Distinguishing Characteristics of Deaf Students and Their Learning Environments

EVERY DAY, 33 BABIES ARE BORN in the United States with some type of hearing loss. Historically, most parents did not find out that their child had a hearing loss until the child was 18 to 30 months old (Yoshinaga-Itano & Apuzzo, 1998). This practice resulted in significant delays in deaf children's language development. In recent years, however, state-mandated early hearing detection and intervention (EHDI) programs have made it possible to screen all babies for hearing loss by one month of age (CDC, 2004). While in 1999 only 25% of babies were screened for hearing loss, by 2004 nearly 90% of babies were being screened for hearing loss (World Council On Hearing Health, 2004). This phenomenal improvement can certainly make a positive impact on the ability of parents and professionals to provide the infant with accessible language at the earliest stage of cognitive development.

While most parents are still mourning the loss of their child's hearing, they are placed under considerable pressure to choose an intervention strategy. Though everyone can agree that immediate access to a rich communication and language environment should be a priority, parents have to choose between conflicting views—often seen more as warring factions—on the best way to communicate with and educate their child. However, with supportive organizations such as the *American Society for Deaf Children, Hands and Voices*, and *Beginnings*, parents can obtain a wealth of information concerning deafness; they can also join supportive networks of other parents of deaf children.

Diversity Within the Deaf Student Population

Deaf children come in complicated packages, full of a multiplicity of interrelated elements. Diversity among the deaf student population seems more complex than in any other population. It encompasses hearing status, communication differences, school placements, additional disabilities, and identities, as well as the common categories of ethnic diversity, social class diversity, cultural diversity, linguistic diversity, and gender diversity (Mudgett-DeCaro, 1997).

Communication and School Placement

Though 50.7% of deaf students use sign language (with or without speech) to communicate in instructional settings, only 26.8% of them have family members who sign regularly in the home. This figure would seem to indicate that a large percentage of deaf students do not have clear communication in the home—a finding of deep concern in the language building of these students.

Students who did not indicate signing as a preferred communication mode communicated through either speech only (47.8%) or cued speech (.3%). It can only be assumed that many of these students fall into the category of hard of hearing.

Deaf and hard of hearing students are educated in a variety of placements. Of the total number of deaf students, 47% are educated in a regular education setting, 29.9% are educated in a self-contained class in regular school settings, 28.1% are educated in a special school or center, 14.1% are educated through a resource room, and 2.6% are educated at home (percent may total more than 100% because of multiple responses).

Not all deaf students who attend public schools receive academic instruction with hearing students. About 64% are integrated for at least part of the week, leaving 36.4% not integrated at all with hearing peers. Some integrated students (25%) use sign language interpreters; others use oral interpreters (1.2%) or cued speech transliterators (0.4%). Integrated students receive a variety of support services, including tutoring (9%), speech training (60.3%), note taking (4.8%), real-time captioning (1.7%), counseling (11.5%), itinerant teacher/services (36.2%), instructional assistants (18.7%), auditory training (26.9%), and occupational physical therapy (9.2%).

Additional Disabilities Conditions

The majority of deaf students do not have additional conditions. However, the percentage of other disabilities is significantly higher for deaf students when compared to the general population of children under age 15. The most notable difference is in the area of mental retardation, where the percentage of mental retardation is more than 10 times that of the general population. Most additional conditions are noted within the deaf population approximately twice as often as in the general population (see Table 6.1).

The limitations that deaf students exhibit on functional assessments give additional insight into the barriers students face in succeeding in a learning environment. Table 6.2 includes all recorded limitations (mild to moderate or severe to profound) in comparison to nondisabled hearing children.

It is important to note that the learning environments of these students are varied. For example, a child's ability to maintain attention to classroom tasks may be influenced by his or her placement in a hearing class without an interpreter. A child's limited ability to engage in appropriate social interaction and classroom behavior also may be a result of an

Table 6.1   Proposed Resilience Program

	Percentage of the deaf population	Percentage of the entire population of children under 15
No additional conditions	57.6	88.8
Low vision	3.3	.6
Legal blindness	1.3	.01
Learning disability	9.2	5.2
Mental retardation	8.2	.9*
ADD/ADHD	6.3	3–5**
Emotional disturbance	1.9	0.9***

Table 6.2   Functional Assessment

Area of limitation in functional assessment	Percentage of deaf and hard of hearing population
Thinking/reasoning	34.6
Maintaining attention to classroom tasks	38.9
Expressive communication	52.7
Receptive communication	53.82
Social interaction / classroom behavior	30.8
Use of hands, arms, and legs	12.4
Balance	10.4
Overall physical health	11.2

inappropriate placement. It does seem clear, though, that communication represents a large deficit in the functional abilities of these students, leaving one to wonder if this finding may reflect more about the suitability of the educational setting and services than about the students being assessed (Karchmer & Allen, 1999). It is also apparent that the inability to maintain attention to classroom tasks and the inability to engage in appropriate social interactions are limitations experienced by a fairly large percentage of deaf students. This finding is significant as we analyze the ability of inclusion settings to meet the communicative needs of deaf students. Interestingly, the areas of greatest limitation are directly related to language and social interactions.

Ethnic and Cultural Diversity

Ethnic and cultural diversity within the community of Deaf learners has surfaced recently as an important area of discussion. Currently, less than 60% of the deaf student population is white. The steady decline in this group is contrasted with a growing percentage of Hispanic and limited English–proficient (LEP) students (Mitchell & Karchmer, 2006). Approximately, 23.7% of deaf students speak and write languages other than English at home. Of this group, 11.7% use Spanish, while 9.4% use multiple languages (Gallaudet Research Institute, January 2005). Not only are these students culturally set apart by being deaf, they also come from ethnically diverse families. These students face the challenge of coping with at least three different cultures—their own ethnic or racial groups, the Deaf community, and the mainstream, which is still predominantly white, middle-class, and hearing (Sass-Lehrer, Gerner de Garcia, and Rovins, 1997). Unfortunately, similar to the academic achievement findings of minority children in the United States, minority deaf children demonstrate significantly lower achievement levels relative to their white deaf peers (Kluwin, 1994, p. 149; Holt, 1997).

Academic Differences

Diversity in ability presents different challenges in educating deaf students. Meeting the needs of the gifted deaf student population becomes possible only after these students have been identified. Yet the common identification procedures rely heavily on the ability to process written English, and they often fail to recognize these students (Valli & Lucas, 1995). Teachers who are accustomed to identifying language and reading problems in deaf children are often geared more toward remediation, not to providing challenging coursework to academically gifted children (Vialle, 1996, p. 259). At the other end of the spectrum lie concerns for accurately identifying learning and other disabilities (Moxley & Loggins, 1991). Since many measures of ability are related to verbal ability and language, these students may also go unnoticed. Many educators will attribute students' low performance levels to deafness instead of further investigating to uncover the source of the difficulty.

Identity Issues

What does it mean to have a Deaf identity? What is the difference between having a Deaf identity and merely being unable to hear? *Deaf identity* is often described as a connection to the Deaf community and sign language, a taking on of the cultural perspective of deafness, instead of a pathological view. In other words, culturally Deaf individuals value deafness positively (Harris, 1995). Other deaf individuals may have a hearing identity or a bicultural identity. Those who identify as having a strong hearing identity tend to communicate orally and did not socialize with many other Deaf people. Those identified as bicultural may come from hearing families and still feel a deep connection to the hearing world, even though they use sign language and may also be connected to the Deaf community (Bat Chava, 2000).

The discussion of diversity in identities is integral to addressing the topic of integrated education because many deaf individuals cite school as the place where they forged their early identities. A person who attends schools where sign language is not used is immersed in a hearing culture and may absorb the view of deafness as a disability (Bat-Chava, 2000). However, a person who experiences signing environments and develops rich communicative relationships may place more value on the deaf experience.

Diversity of hearing loss also has a profound effect on the needs, identities, and communication modes and educational achievement of students (Powers, 2003). One specific category has a history of being overlooked— hard of hearing students. Children with "mild" or "moderate" hearing losses may melt into regular classrooms only to be considered as aggressive, impulsive, or inattentive (Meadow-Orlans, Mertens, & Sass-Lehrer, 2003; Meyer, 2003). Only later are these behaviors diagnosed as symptoms of hearing loss. The delayed recognition of actual hearing loss may result in parent (and teacher) guilt over punishing the child for not listening. Hard of hearing children learn amazing coping strategies that help them to blend in with hearing students. By using visual cues in their environment, students are at times able to make up for what they don't hear (Vesey & Wilson, 2003).

Hard of hearing people often struggle with a self-identity that is caught between two worlds—the hearing world and the deaf world (Vesey and Wilson, 2003). They are neither deaf nor hearing, and they are also both deaf and hearing (Silver, 2003). While the hearing world characterizes them as deaf, the deaf world characterizes them as hearing. In the past, deaf and hard of hearing people tended to be educated together, but with the advent of technology, a split has occurred not only in placement, but also in identity. Many hard of hearing students are left without a strong identity and spend much of their time trying to fit in with the dominant culture. This view of "fitting in" seems to be admired among many hearing people who "believe that the greatest success of a person with a hearing loss is to live—or at least pass—everyday as a hearing person" (Vesey & Wilson, 2003, p. 13).

Children with mild or moderate hearing loss almost always attend public school, but they may not receive the support or accommodations that they need (Meyer, 2003). "The hard work of listening—the act of receiving pieces of sound, resolving ambiguities, and filling the missing holes—is hard work" (Vesey & Wilson, 2003, p. 4). For hearing students, classrooms are language-rich environments, but for students with mild or moderate hearing loss, the classroom can be very large and noisy (Meyer, 2003). When a class of children and their teacher value competitive, highly verbal learning situations, the hard of hearing child placed in that room becomes isolated, even though he is in the mainstream. "The concept of mainstreaming will work when hard of hearing children view themselves as part of the mainstream" (Barton, 1977, p. 19).

In light of the diverse complexities found within the deaf student population, it is not enough to aim for a solution based on one set of variables. Instead, as educators of the deaf guide students toward academic achievement, they will have to take into account the role of the differences in those students. The paramount goal must be that policy, placements, and classroom practices support, rather than suppress, the individual student's needs and desires.

Part 2

The Research Study

Voices of Deaf Children

7

ALL VOICES ARE VALUABLE IN UNDERSTANDING the complexities of deaf students' experiences in integrated settings. For this reason, I interviewed deaf students, interpreters, deaf education teachers, and regular education teachers. In this and the following chapters, I have included all quotes relating to each specific category, as well as an interpretation of the emerging themes. Each participant created a new name for himself or herself. These names are used throughout the chapters so readers may follow the path of a single participant. It is important to note that not all students responded to each topic. The participants were allowed to guide the conversation and, therefore, were treated as conversational partners instead of objects of research. By asking probing questions aligned with the research questions, I was able to narrow the focus. Overall, it seemed that this approach was extremely effective, giving the participants more comfort in sharing liberally on topics that interested them.

The deaf student participants range in age from 10 to 18 years, and they reside in Pennsylvania, Maryland, and Ohio. All of them have hearing parents. They share a common experience of being educated in integrated classrooms that are located in larger suburban school districts. All deaf student participants also share the common experience of receiving an interpreted education through a sign language interpreter. At the time of the interviews three of the students were experiencing their first year at a school for the deaf, after spending years in integrated classrooms. Though all the students can communicate through ASL, two of them communicate in the integrated classroom through voice only, but they still use an interpreter to receive and to clarify information.

As I analyzed the responses of the students, a dividing line seemed to emerge between the students that exhibit some ability to hear and speak and the students who are profoundly deaf and only communicate through sign language. This dividing line is so prevalent throughout this data that

I will refer to the first group as the signing deaf students (those students using *only* sign language to communicate) and the second group as the speaking deaf students (even though they may use signs to some extent). The participants in each group are listed below.

Signing deaf students	Speaking deaf students
Zack	Tyler
Kyle	Kaitlyn
Jasmine	Leslie
Julie	Patrick
Ashley	Sam

It is important to note that these categorical references are based on the students' *preferred* method of communicating, not on an enforced teaching philosophy. Also it is important to note that the speaking abilities of these speaking deaf students represent a wide range of intelligibility. Most of these speaking students vocalize with a "deaf voice," which is markedly different from that of a hearing student's voice. Also, all speaking deaf students know ASL and use it to some extent to communicate.

Four of the student participants have cochlear implants. However, the experience of having a cochlear implant did not seem to directly lead to a common communication strategy or perspective. One of the students with a cochlear implant uses only signs to communicate, and therefore is considered in the deaf signing group, while the others are considered speaking deaf students. Table 7.1 provides further information about the student participants.

Presentation of Themes From Deaf Student Interviews

The students' responses have been organized by topics: After each topic, an interpretive section discusses the themes emerging within these responses. The final interpretive section presents a collective discussion of the major themes found throughout the deaf student interviews. In the presentation of the themes, the responses have been organized in the following manner: general feelings about school, about interpreters, and about building relationships in a hearing school, as well as unexpected findings.

Narrative Sketches of the Deaf Students

Zack: Zack loves to play tag and tell jokes. Though he is profoundly deaf, he often chooses to not wear hearing aids. Instead, he prefers to be identified

Table 7.1   Characteristics of Deaf Student Participants

	Age	Grade	Cochlear implant	Primary mode of communication	Experienced both hearing schools and deaf schools
Zack	10	4		ASL	X
Kyle	10	4		ASL	X
Tyler	11	5	X	ASL/Voice	
Kaitlyn	13	7		ASL/Voice	
Leslie	14	8	X	Voice	
Jasmine	15	9		ASL	X
Julie	15	9	X	ASL	X
Patrick	15	9		ASL/Voice	
Ashley	18	10		ASL	
Sam	18	10	X	Voice	

with the deaf community and communicate solely through his native language of ASL. During the interview in his home, he seemed comfortable and relaxed but was anxious to resume his game of Nintendo. His mother shared that he had been placed in a deaf preschool program and then moved to an integrated school for first through fourth grade. This year, he chose to go back to the school for the deaf for fifth grade. His mother explained that while Zack was in preschool, he had been considered a leader, but after moving to an integrated classroom, he became quiet and withdrawn. In fact, the teachers often claimed that he "didn't say a word." This year, after he went back to the school for the deaf, Zack's mother has seen a complete change in his personality. He is back to being talkative at school and home. Once again, he is a leader among his peers, and seems more self-confident.

Kyle: Kyle clearly enjoys playing with his friends at the school for the deaf. He was diagnosed at age 2 with a profound hearing loss in both ears and soon after began his education at an oral school for the deaf. He attended 4 years there before being enrolled in the public school system's mainstream program. During the first year, Kyle learned sign language and was mainstreamed for two classes. In second and third grade, he was in the hearing classroom with an interpreter most of the day. Kyle lives with his grandmother, who describes him as a very social child and a leader. She explains that most of the time he is friendly and fun, though he can be manipulative and have a short temper. She also shares that he has a very low frustration level and a high energy level. Even though she encourages him to learn to use his voice, she also encourages him to learn sign language and to explore deaf culture. Overall, Kyle is a caring and loving child who has many interests. According to his grandmother, "He is basically a very happy little boy."

Tyler: With self-confidence, Tyler approached the interview process with anticipation. His ability to easily interact with both deaf and hearing students makes him a popular friend among both groups. Tyler has a cochlear implant and is able to speak intelligibly. His parents learned sign language when Tyler was young, and they still use it at times for clarification.

Kaitlyn: Kaitlyn loves to go shopping. Though she is quiet and somewhat withdrawn in school, she is friendly and bouncy when at home or with deaf friends. Kaitlyn uses her voice to communicate both at school and at home. Her speech is fairly intelligible, especially for those who know her well.

Leslie: Leslie functions very much like a hearing student. Her increasing ability to identify sounds through her cochlear implant has led her to being able to use the phone and to speak clearly. Though others may think of her as "hearing" or perhaps "hard of hearing," she again and again refers to herself as "deaf." Leslie has grown up in mainstream programs and now requires very little assistance to succeed in the classroom. Leslie is exuberant, confident, and friendly, and she seems to enjoy being involved in school and interacting with her friends. Leslie used her voice to respond to questions in the interview. While doing so, she gives an interesting view of what it is like to be considered a successful cochlear implant recipient in a hearing school.

Jasmine: Jasmine is a high-school freshman at a school for the deaf. Her delicate and pretty features are in contrast to the strong views and emotion that she portrays. Jasmine's deaf education began at a school for the deaf, where she was educated from age 5 to age 7. She then was transferred to an integrated school, where she completed first through eighth grade. This year was her first year back in a school for the deaf. Her mother talked of the growing loneliness that Jasmine faced while being educated in a mainstream program until she was nearly suicidal. During her years in mainstream classes, Jasmine often wrote stories and poems with themes of isolation, alienation, and death. By the eighth grade, not only were her parents worried about her mental stability, but they also saw a nosedive in her motivation to learn. As a last resort, they sent her back to a school for the deaf. Her mother reports that in the past few months, Jasmine has transformed into a motivated student, a social butterfly, and a girl that is in love with life. "She makes us laugh every day. It is good to see her smile."

Julie: Julie was interviewed in her home, where she was open and friendly. She seemed to look forward to the interview and had thought of several ideas she wanted to share. According to her mother, Julie is very outgoing and has a take-charge attitude. Her athletic success in soccer has earned her a great deal of respect from the student body. During the interview, Julie seemed confident and relaxed while giving a very poignant view of life as the only deaf student in a regular education high school. Julie attended a school for the deaf for first grade, but moved to an integrated program for second through fifth grade. In sixth grade, she again tried the school for the deaf but felt that she had become the subject of harassment by the other deaf students. She again transferred back into a public school for middle school and high school. At the time of this interview, she was the only deaf student in a very large high school. Julie chose to have a cochlear implant when she was 13, and she now says that she loves it. She explains that she mostly likes the fact that it helps her to hear environmental sounds, such as the phone ringing, the bell at school, and a car coming down the street. But recently, she has started to enjoy music and is able to differentiate between voices of people she knows.

Patrick: Patrick is well known for his friendly personality and his sparkling sense of humor. Patrick's positive outlook is noted throughout the interview as he frames difficult issues in a positive light and follows them with a quick smile. Patrick communicates through a combined approach of speech and signing. Patrick lives with his mother who has learned to sign and is active in advocating for the rights of deaf children in the community. Patrick has grown up in the mainstream setting of a large suburban school district. He seems content with his educational environment. Patrick is fully mainstreamed in a high school where two other deaf students also attend.

Sam: Sam is anxiously awaiting her high school graduation, which is scheduled to take place 5 days after her interview. Sam seems independent and highly confident and is excited about her plans to attend a state university in the fall. Her hopes are to succeed in the medical program and become a nurse, following in the footsteps of her mother and grandmother. Although Sam was born profoundly deaf, she had a cochlear implant at the age of 3 years. She explained that the cochlear implant failed at age 8, but she recently had another cochlear implant. She has grown up identifying herself as a hard of hearing individual. Sam's speech is intelligible, and she feels this has helped her to succeed in the hearing world.

Ashley: Ashley is the only deaf student in a large suburban high school. She prefers to use American Sign Language to communicate, but she is also fluent in cued speech. She describes her independent streak as being expressed by living on her own. It seems the pierced tongue may also be an extension of this independence. Her demeanor is confident and friendly, and she stops several times during the interview to chat with friends who are frequently calling her on her Sidekick pager. Ashley has been in an integrated public school from kindergarten through twelfth grade, but she mentions that she has moved from school to school, particularly in her younger years.

General Feelings About School

Loneliness and Isolation

What is it like to be a deaf student in a hearing school? What does it feel like?

Zack

It was only so-so . . . I didn't really like it. I remember being embarrassed and a little frightened in the hearing school.

Kyle

I didn't really like the hearing school because I couldn't communicate with the hearing kids. I'd try to talk with them sometimes, but mostly I was just shy. I felt lower then them, so I usually didn't even try.

Kaitlyn

I'm just friends with the deaf kids. Well, I'm not the only deaf kid in the school, so I'm not so lonely as those who can't talk. Learn to speak. If you can talk, it is much better.

Tyler

I feel OK and comfortable about going to a hearing school.

Leslie

Sometimes I feel lonely, like if people talk a million miles an hour. I just sit there and listen to them. I just like to listen a lot.

But, I think it is fun going to school now. I have a lot of friends, and I just feel normal. It is just that when I was little I didn't really have many friends and I really didn't want to go to school. Just being myself helped, I guess.

Jasmine

I know it was a good school for the hearing kids, but it is hard for deaf people to understand and learn there. I feel left out because I'm deaf . . . where's my culture? I'm closed in, contained, but not in my own culture. I never experienced [socializing] at the hearing school. That's why I never learned.

If you don't have anyone to talk with at school and you come home and you don't have anyone to talk to at home, then you can get real lonely and just give up. You'll feel like you're not learning anything.

Julie

I think it's the environment. It's just a cold, less-friendly environment. The school seems cold, not too friendly. I look forward to getting home.

Sometimes, I'm lonely. I'm on my own, the only deaf kid in the school so I have to live with that. I'm lonely when I feel I am struggling in school. When I feel all alone, then I lose my motivation—it just kind of bottoms out.

Ashley

When I was younger, I felt I could join and interact with any group, but as I got older, I felt more distance, more isolation from hearing kids. At the time, it didn't really bother me; I got used to it as it happened. I really thought it was just the environment I was in, that it really wasn't anything important.

Sam

I like going to a hearing school. I feel I have gotten a good education there. And I've learned how to live in the hearing culture. But I want to learn more about the deaf culture.

When deaf students were asked about school, they exclusively answered from a social perspective, rather than from an academic perspective. Interestingly, this differed from the adult participants, who answered almost exclusively from an academic perspective.

When reflecting on their feelings about school, the speaking deaf students tended to respond somewhat positively. However, the comments from the signing deaf students revealed deeper negative feelings. The younger signing students gave short, but insightful answers that told of their misery in school. Zack and Kyle both seemed to feel that the communication barrier was so intense that they could not glean any enjoyment in being there. Julie also revealed very negative feelings toward school. She linked these negative feelings to a cold school climate. Looking beyond individuals, Julie saw the problem as a school-wide problem, a general lack of friendliness.

With insight, Jasmine acknowledges the value of her school for hearing students, but she also recognizes its limitations as a place for her to learn. Jasmine's comments demonstrate a difference in how the hearing students might benefit, in comparison to how she sees herself benefiting. These comments show a deeper perception of the divide between the school's ability to provide a good education for hearing students and its ability to provide a good education for deaf students. Jasmine's viewpoint that her school is a "good school for hearing kids" seems to be a sharp contrast to her inward view of a lack of success for herself.

This alarming consensus of negative feelings among the signing deaf students is a stark comparison to the more positive positions of speaking deaf students. But even within speaking students' comments you see a hint of being unsettled, either in a longing to connect with the deaf community or a memory of not being accepted. It is interesting that Leslie has seen a change in the way she views school from her early years, when she did not have many friends and did not want to go to school, to now, when she is older and is having fun in school. Perhaps this change was prompted by her increasing ability to produce and understand speech with her cochlear implant. However, Leslie attributes the change to feeling comfortable with herself. Sam also expressed general positive feelings for her school but reveals a need to connect with deaf culture. She seems to be searching for her cultural roots while still supporting her integrated past.

When one reflects on the responses concerning general feelings about school, it does not seem surprising that a divide exists between the signing deaf students and the speaking deaf students. The signing deaf students experience a stronger communication barrier than those who can communicate directly with others in their environment. The signing deaf students may also experience a greater feeling of alienation. Kaitlyn grasps the core of this underlying phenomenon when she emphasizes that "if you can talk, it is much better." Overall, the responses from this interview question suggest that signing deaf students hold significantly more negative feelings toward their hearing schools than their speaking deaf counterparts.

Loneliness and isolation were haunting themes that emerged in the interviews again and again. Though this theme was found in the responses of students from both the signing and the speaking group, it seemed much stronger among the signing deaf students. Kaitlyn seemed to understand this increased depth of loneliness for the students who could not speak when she said, "I'm not so lonely as those who can't talk."

In each interview of signing deaf students, a glimpse of the loneliness was revealed. In Zack's interview, he repeatedly shared the embarrassment that he felt in his elementary hearing classroom. He mentioned several times that he felt "different" and that it was embarrassing to him. Perhaps this is why his mother described him as being very quiet in school. Though Kyle doesn't use the term *embarrassing*, he does say that he was *shy* because of his lack of ability to communicate with the other students. He also shares that he felt *lower* than the other students, making him less enthusiastic to communicate. This feeling of being inferior is echoed in the responses of several other students in the signing group. Ashley talks about the isolation enveloping her as she grew older. At the time, she felt this was normal, but now she looks back and realizes it was significant.

Julie and Jasmine both acknowledge the devastating link between loneliness and the ability to learn. Their combined viewpoint seems to suggest that students who feel lonely are unable to maintain the motivation to learn, which leads to lower academic achievement. In recognizing this link, they confirm the critical need to support the social side of learning.

Jasmine links her loneliness and lack of academic success to the larger issue of being detached from her culture. Therefore, it seems that loneliness can be expressed both from an individual perspective and from a cultural perspective. Sam also confirmed this when she expressed a longing to know more of deaf culture.

In contrast, Tyler and Patrick (both speaking deaf students) did not mention loneliness or isolation in their interviews. Interestingly, they spoke quite positively about their school environments and told me of their "many friends." However, when I interviewed the teacher of one of the boys who gave a glowing report of many positive relationships with peers and teachers, she described him as quiet, withdrawn, and lonely in school, and she said he rarely interacted with anyone. It is possible that the student's definition of positive relationships is based on actions less rich than normal hearing peer relationships.

Leslie is a speaking deaf student, and yet she did experience loneliness and feeling different. Though hearing through her cochlear implant and her ability to lipread usually served her well, she still felt left out when people were talking quickly, and she couldn't understand. Interestingly, she chose to just enjoy the passive stance of listening, instead of trying to join a conversation she was not understanding.

With loneliness and isolation a major theme among the deaf student participants, it is important to explore the ramifications of these deeply felt emotions. What are the consequences of long-term loneliness? An abundance of research has been conducted on the topic of loneliness. Though much of the research has focused extensively been on the reasons for loneliness, more recent research has looked closer at the outcomes of loneliness, clearly linking loneliness to other behavioral and emotional problems (Kupersmidt, Sigda, Sedikides, and Voegler, 1999). The range of emotional problems associated with loneliness includes low self-esteem, depression, and social anxiety. Certain social problems, such as peer rejection, victimization, and lack of high-quality friendships, are closely identified with loneliness. Additional behavioral problems such as shyness, social withdrawal, spending more time alone, lack of dating relationships, and decreased participation in religious and extracurricular school activities have also been linked to loneliness (Kupersmidt et al., 1999). Perlman and Landolt (1999) also reported links between loneliness and other problems such as physical illness, suicide, alcohol use, poor psychological adjustment, aggression, low grades in school, stealing, and vandalism. An online survey of 353 self-described lonely participants revealed even greater consequences, including a fascination with death, feelings of hate, and cold and empty feelings void of emotion (Seepersad, 1997). The dangers of feeling lonely may be even greater among adolescents, who may use ineffective coping strategies to try and dispel these feelings. Rubenstein and Shaver (1982) reported that adolescents were the loneliest of all of the age groups and often coped with their loneliness through sad passivity (sleeping, taking tranquilizers, eating, and doing nothing). Other researchers have found that loneliness can cause medical problems (Harms, 2000) and other serious problems such as turning to crime, self-induced isolation, and exaggerated consumption of medication (Rokach, 1998).

Deaf students may be particularly vulnerable to loneliness, which can be elicited by isolation, not having close friends, and not identifying with or not being accepted by valued social groups (Cacioppo, 1999), treating loneliness as an objective state brought about by objective circumstances, rather than a subjective state brought about by other subjective states. Since all three experiences were distinctly described by the deaf students interviewed, it is reasonable to conclude that deaf students in hearing schools are strongly susceptible to loneliness and the associated conditions that might be related to it.

In fact, several of these symptoms were noted by the parents of deaf students. For example, Jasmine's mother expressed her concern that Jasmine would sleep for hours and had become obsessed with death. The fear of Jasmine's suicidal tendencies led her parents to find another educational program for her. When she was placed in the deaf school, these symptoms vanished, and now her parents describe her as "in love with life."

Zack's mother spoke of his intense quietness both at school and at home during his years in a mainstream program. She also described an intense personality change (from being a leader to being withdrawn), as he entered the mainstream school, and another change (from a quiet child to an outgoing and talkative child) later, as he returned to a deaf school.

Overcoming loneliness is not so much dependent on the number of relationships one makes as it is on the quality and depth of the relationships (Tucker-Ladd, 1996). Based on this perspective, it is vital for deaf students to develop relationships with several other students to ward off the possible consequences of loneliness. While some students may not experience loneliness in a hearing educational environment, educators and parents should carefully monitor deaf children for these possible indicators while finding ways to expose them to meaningful quality relationships.

Struggling With Inferiority and Lack of Power

How do you feel in your hearing school?

Themes of inferiority and a lack of power run through many of the responses to the questions. Though the students used different terms to describe it, many of them identified it as a major frustration of an integrated education.

Kyle

I'd try to talk with them sometimes, but mostly I was just shy. I felt lower then them, so I usually didn't even try.

Jasmine

Some hearing people think deaf people can't do anything. But I put up with them. I feel like uniforms at school. Uniforms, meaning all the hearing people control the deaf people.

Hearing people try to make deaf interested in hearing things . . . come on with us, we'll teach you to talk, use your hearing aid and try to hear us. I don't have patience for that. What about my culture?

Julie

Yeah . . . I mean some of the hearing students are idiots. They prove themselves by their actions . . . they don't understand what it means to be deaf. I mean, some of them are just plain stupid, but I don't let them get to me.

Ashley

Being deaf in a hearing school, I found that sometimes the other kids thought less of me. For example they might be sitting around a table and whispering to each other and I'd actually catch what they had said to each other by lipreading them. They thought I couldn't lipread, and some deaf people can, other deaf people can't. Really, they just kept showing their surprise that deaf people can do so many things . . . which means that they thought deaf people can't do them in the first place. I say the only thing a deaf person can't do is hear, that's all.

These feelings of inferiority and lack of power were evident in most of the deaf student's comments, whether they were in the signing or the speaking group. Some of the inferiority came embedded within the students themselves. Kyle shared that he felt "lower" than the other students, so he was shy. Zack spoke often of his feelings of embarrassment and shyness. He explained that these feelings were intensified when he felt "stuck" in the communication process.

Some of the feelings of inferiority originated from outside sources, such as the hearing teachers' lower expectations for the deaf students than for their other students. Sam specifically spoke of this happening in her school. Even with her mother's determination in repeatedly addressing this issue, Sam still felt the teachers held lower expectations for her. Julie also alluded to this problem when she stated that she did not always answer the teacher's questions because she did not have to.

A perception of inferiority came from the hearing students, as well. They seemed to think that deaf students were not capable. Ashley's comments in particular expressed a frustration in the hearing students' *surprise* that she could do things. Julie's comments alluded to the harassment that she had endured due to other students treating her as if she were inferior.

Some of the deaf students blamed their inferior treatment on cultural oppression. Jasmine's thoughts revealed a sense that she has been forced to assimilate and others do not respect her language and culture. This need for a culturally competent educational approach is echoed in the comments of other students, as well.

A few deaf students felt a lack of power in dealing with interpreters. Clearly, they did not see the interpreters as allies. For example, one deaf student remarked, "They earn money. They just take advantage of deaf people by earning money working with them." If deaf students do not see the interpreter as an ally, they may tend to believe the interpreter is either aligned the teacher or is working for self-interest. Interpreters who are not involved with the deaf community outside of school walls may perpetuate this kind of viewpoint. Jasmine's litmus test for interpreters seems to be "if you align yourself with hearing culture, you can't really be my ally."

Most students, especially adolescents, feel powerless in school. They cannot choose their teachers, classmates, curriculum, or school. And all students are involved in numerous relationships in which they are the one with less power. However, for deaf students, this lack of power is more intense. While hearing students can choose their friends, deaf students are often stuck with whoever chooses to learn sign language. While hearing students can exercise some control over their interaction with others, deaf students are severely limited and must rely heavily on the interpreter. Though hearing students often can work harder to achieve a better education, deaf students are limited by many factors, such as the effectiveness of their interpreters, their ability to interact with the curriculum, and the level of support services available. While most hearing students can gain support and advice on addressing their struggles at home, deaf students rarely have anyone at home who can communicate with them at that level.

The lack of power for deaf students seems to extend far beyond that of other groups of students with disabilities or from those from culturally diverse backgrounds because it is inherently connected to communication access.

Deaf people have long been subjected to a lack of power. But the long history of forced oralism seems to now have turned into a new history of forced assimilation in hearing schools—without the tools to support success. Some deaf students seem so accustomed to this situation that they do not notice. But the deaf students who have experienced the language-rich environments of deaf schools show a sense of empowerment. A prevalent theme throughout Zack, Kyle, and Jasmine's interviews involves multiple comparisons of the lack of power felt in hearing schools and the sense of empowerment gained through their experiences at the deaf school. These three students are highly aware of the oppressive nature of the language deprivation at hearing schools and highly supportive of the increase in power that is afforded them in the language-rich environment found in deaf schools.

Change

How have you experienced social change as you've gotten older?

Several of the students experienced a change in their level of satisfaction as they grew older. Julie and Ashley, both deaf signing students, seemed to experience more alienation as they grew older. However, Leslie, a speaking deaf student, felt more acceptance.

Leslie
I think it is fun going to school now. I have a lot of friends, and I just feel normal. It is just that when I was little I didn't really have many friends and I really didn't want to go to school. Just being myself helped, I guess.

Julie
I went to hearing schools. In elementary school I had good friends, and I enjoyed my social interaction at school. The teachers were learning some sign language and fingerspelling. Then later in middle school I was even more motivated to work hard. . . . I felt close and connected there. The people at the school seemed to have an understanding of deaf culture, such as making things more visual, and the struggles we have with written language. Middle school was no problem, everything was fine. In high school they are more strict, less flexible; more cold, less friendly.

Ashley

When I was growing up I had a very positive attitude toward hearing people. I could basically get along with anyone. As I got older, I felt more distance, more isolation from hearing kids. At the time, it didn't really bother me; I got used to it as it happened. I really thought it was just the environment I was in, that it really wasn't anything important. But then, about the time I got into sixth grade, I began to become interested in the Deaf community and started to have less patience for hearing people. . . . My feelings started to change. Once I understood the ease of communication among deaf people, I sensed a change in my personality . . . at least regarding hearing people. I wasn't able to be as active or involved with hearing people, and I didn't enjoy just being passive and quiet, so I don't bother with hearing people so much anymore. I will say, however, that it did provide a good challenge for me to go to a hearing school because it forced me to interact with hearing people and that has its benefits, like for my future employment, for example.

Some deaf students may experience more frustration as they mature in the school system, while others might find more acceptance. For signing deaf students, though, the change in the way students socialize may affect the level of interaction they have with that social circle. While hearing students are moving away from playground games and toward intricate social systems of "who likes who," the deaf students may feel more and more alienated. In Ashley's experience, the isolation began when she discovered the deaf community—a group of people with whom she shared a language and could easily identify herself. However, it seems possible that the isolation had been a part of her life before that time, and it was only at that time that she discovered what she had been missing. This sense of awareness has not yet reached the other deaf students. If you do not know anything could be different, than you may be less likely to be frustrated with the system and more likely to believe that your feelings of alienation are normal.

From Julie and Ashley's comments, one might assume that younger deaf children have a more positive social experience. However, the youngest participants, Zack and Kyle, both described in vivid detail their misery and frustrations in social relationships at the elementary level.

While Julie and Ashley's social experiences became worse as they grew older, Leslie felt her social experiences were improving. However, it was during this time that Leslie became increasingly more capable of communicating clearly through speech and listening. Again, perhaps this is indicative of the benefit of being able to speak and communicate directly with others within the school environment.

Interpreters

The Qualities of a Good Interpreter

What makes an interpreter good?

During the conversational interviews with deaf students, the students spoke freely of their relationships with interpreters and the interpreter qualities that they felt were most important to them.

Kyle

I had a good interpreter . . . Karen . . . I really liked her. I thought of her as a friend.

Tyler

It's really important to me to have a good relationship with my interpreter. [It's also important] for the interpreter to translate every word, so I can understand clearly.

Leslie

I know in elementary school, I had [an interpreter] and she was like my friend. We just really connected, and we got along very well. She knew what I needed, and I knew what she needed. So I think basically it is key that you talk to each other.

I don't think interpreters should just strictly be professional and never talk to the kids, and I think the kids should be able to talk to the interpreter without feeling uncomfortable.

Jasmine

Interpreters should do their work their way. Some interpreters are friends with the deaf students, I don't know, but I don't think it makes it any more enjoyable.

Julie

They can't be stuck up or be such a nit-picking professional. They need to have a normal body type, not way over weight. They need to have a cool personality, not strict or overbearing, telling me what I can and can't do. They need to be emotionally stable—I mean, not really shy or embarrassed to speak up and comfortable in their surroundings—not nervous or obsessive about everything being perfect.

For example, my interpreter got hit by a ball once in gym class and she didn't blow up or get mad about it. My interpreter and I are pretty close. She and I talk a lot. Actually the three of us, including the deaf education teacher, are really close and work well together. We do a lot of fun things together, maybe more than we really should, but I really enjoy being able to work so well together with them.

Patrick

My interpreter is pretty cool. She likes to joke around a lot, so I like that kind of interpreter. She is pretty good.

Ashley

I had a different interpreter nearly every school year. Sometimes they were flexible and friendly and easy to get along with; other interpreters were more strict and reserved . . . they were more difficult to work with. The perfect interpreter would be one that was flexible, aware of different ways to communicate, and knowledgeable about deaf culture. Not just a signer, but someone who knows about deaf culture.

In the field of interpreting, the focus has been on interpreter skill. It is generally assumed that the skill level of the interpreter is the indicator of what makes someone a good interpreter. However, in these interviews a very different theme emerges. Interestingly, nearly all of the students interviewed identified social skills as an important factor. They also mentioned personality, physical appearance, skill, and cultural competency.

Do the majority of deaf students not regard skill as important? While it seems highly unlikely, their emphasis on the interpreter's social skills may represent their ability to survive in the highly charged social environment of school. It also would support the theory that the deaf students see the interpreter as an extension of themselves. This extension theory contends that the extent to which the interpreter is accepted socially by the hearing peers and by the hearing teacher directly influences the extent to which the deaf student will be accepted. The deaf students may develop very strong opinions about the mannerisms, personality, and clothes of their interpreter because they feel these factors directly reflect on their social acceptance within the school. This extension theory is discussed further in the next section.

The collective opinion of the students interviewed also suggests a friendship relationship with their interpreter as being most effective. In fact, not one student shared a concern that the interpreter maintain a more distant professional relationship. In contrast, the students described *good* interpreters as those who were fun, friendly, and approachable. Julie, in particular, seemed to revel in the fun working and playing relationship she has with both her interpreter and her deaf education teacher. She found joy in their closeness and mentioned that they do lots of fun things together, but curiously, she adds, "more than we probably should." In the interview, Julie seemed particularly upbeat when speaking of her relationship with her interpreter and deaf education teacher. She directly attributes her success in high school to their close relationship. Jasmine, however, insisted that even friendly interpreters did not make an integrated education enjoyable.

Ashley expressed the need for interpreters to be more than just signers. She insisted that interpreters need to know and understand deaf culture in order to be effective. To her, it is this cultural understanding and competency that serves as the basis for not only effective communication but also effective relationship building.

This call for friendship harkens back to the themes that emerged from the 1995 New Orleans Allies Conference, held in Nashua, New Hampshire. The conference brought together facets of the deaf community and the interpreters who served them. The issue of power was expressed through a perspective of allies. The deaf community seemed to say, "Either you are our ally, or you are an ally to the hearing person. But it is impossible for you to be neutral." From this conference, a resulting discussion was sparked in the interpreting field, a sociopolitical discussion of whose side the interpreter is on.

The deaf students in the study are saying to interpreters, "Be our allies. We need you on our side." Clearly, the interpreters who were seen as allies were also seen as most effective.

Describe your favorite kind of interpreter.

The deaf students had a strong understanding of the social impact of their interpreter. When asked to describe the perfect interpreter, they answered as follows:

Zack
Well, there aren't any men interpreters . . . they are all women, so it's kind of embarrassing.

Kyle
I guess I liked the ones that were younger.

Kaitlyn
She would be young and *fun*!

Jasmine

It's important that the interpreter sign what people are saying. . . . I don't care what the interpreter looks like. Interpreters can't be stuck up; they should teach people signs and about the right ways to interact with Deaf people.

Julie

Who the interpreter is determines how much social interaction I get. If the other kids don't feel comfortable around her, they aren't going to talk to me. My interpreter is good. She's cool, I like her personality. She's very fluent, doesn't wear fancy professional clothes, just normal comfortable clothes, you know normal stuff for the adults in the building. I mean it is still appropriate. One day she wore this annoying patterned shirt and that was funny, I thought it was funny, anyway. But she's very good, skilled, and fluent. She's not the most advanced interpreter on the planet, but I think she's very good.

My interpreter needs to have a similar personality, to kind of act like me. That's real important. Like I enjoy teasing and joking with my interpreter and she can dish it back to me as good as I can give it. I enjoy that.

Patrick

I like interpreters who have a good sense of humor. That is really important to me! I guess I prefer interpreters who are younger. Not those that are heading for retirement and have lost their motivation.

⸺━◆━⸺

When asked to describe the perfect interpreter, the students noted characteristics that they themselves had. Zack wanted a male interpreter because he found it embarrassing to have a woman interpreter. Kaitlyn and Zack both wanted an interpreter who was young. Julie went into much detail about the desired personality and physical appearance of an interpreter. Interestingly, she insisted that her interpreter have a "similar personality" and "kind of act like me." This desire for an interpreter to "be like me" may suggest the extent to which the students see the interpreter as an extension of themselves—the extension theory. When asked how the interpreter affected their experience in school, several students noted that the interpreter's physical appearance and personality directly affected the extent to which their peers included them.

The flip side of this perspective is that interpreters who are older, less enthusiastic, and do not fit into the student culture serve as a barrier to the social integration of deaf students. As one student protested, "On the first day of school I worry about who my interpreter will be. Yuk . . . if she is ugly and fat, no one will *ever* talk to me!"

And yet some students still recognize that it is important for the interpreter to be skilled in the interpreting process. Tyler wanted his interpreter to thoroughly interpret the message and not leave anything out. He understands that this is the only way for him to succeed academically in the classroom. Jasmine felt strongly that interpreter skill was important, as was the ability to serve as an advocate for deaf people. However, from her cultural perspective, she thought that some interpreters were stuck up—perhaps implying that they did not serve her as an ally. The unexpected finding of the deaf students' interviews is their emphasis on the social considerations of age, clothing, and personality, rather than skill.

Extension Theory

A normal characteristic of adolescence is the development of an enhanced awareness of self and the ability to reflect on one's own being. Because of the many noticeable physical changes of adolescence, this self-awareness often turns into self-consciousness, with an accompanying feeling of awkwardness. Adolescent children often develop a preoccupation with physical appearance and attractiveness, with a heightened sensitivity to differences from peers (Merk, 2003) This self concept of body becomes influential in how adolescents relate to themselves and to each other. This internal representation or body image is intimately linked to the relationships that the adolescent maintains (Cordeiro, 2005).

Hearing students may notice the unattractive physical characteristics of their teachers, doctors, parents, and other adults, but they do not seem personally affected by them. Deaf students, however, have a unique relationship with their interpreters. The interpreter serves as a social representative, and, therefore, the interpreter's image is directly tied to the deaf adolescents' physical self image. Since the physical image of the interpreter merges with the student's own preoccupation with his or her self-image, the student has a heightened awareness of and may be embarrassed by the interpreter's physical appearance.

Interestingly, deaf students noticed that when they were served by less attractive interpreters, their social interactions were more limited.

Therefore, it seems that hearing students also merged the identities of the student with the interpreter.

An Interpreted Education

What is it like to learn through an interpreted education? Who do you ask if you don't understand? How does it make you feel to have an interpreter in the classroom signing to you, while everyone else is learning directly? The students shared interesting insights into these questions, which are at the core of learning in an integrated setting.

Zack

> What would you do if you didn't understand? I'd ask the interpreter. But a lot of the times with the interpreter I still didn't understand what I was supposed to do. I got embarrassed if everyone was looking at me. I prefer it when people aren't looking at me. So I don't know. At the deaf school I ask the teacher and the teacher can explain it, so I know what to do. I think it was hard to understand the interpreter. People would speak fast, but the interpreter was slow. All the other kids would be finished first; I'd always be last. I had to finish writing before I went to lunch or outside to play.

Kyle

> If I didn't understand the work we were doing, like if I didn't understand the directions, I'd sometimes ask the interpreter, and if the interpreter didn't know what to do, then I'd ask the teacher. I had an interpreter in the classroom, but I didn't like having to look back and forth between the interpreter and the other stuff happening in the classroom.

Tyler

> If I don't understand a question in class, the interpreter will explain it to me. But a hearing school needs a strong hearing support teacher to teach deaf students.

Jasmine

> Hearing teachers try to explain, they lecture . . . but at the deaf school they make eye contact. We will learn by doing first and then write about it, which is easy because we just experienced it. Hearing people can just talk about it and then start writing. In deaf school we know what to write because first we see, touch, and manipulate things. Deaf people are visual learners, and we need to touch and manipulate to learn, and if you have questions you can ask and get immediate responses. Hearing people are more auditory learners and can learn just by hearing. It's hard for deaf people in hearing schools. They don't give many visual examples in hearing schools. You just get a paper and you are left wondering how to answer . . . so either you copy from someone else or you fail.

If I had my way, I wouldn't want to have an interpreter. Just teach me directly in ASL.

Julie

I struggle to understand some of the teachers. The hearing students do OK with the teachers, but for a deaf student, it is different; it is harder. The homework is based on written paragraphs, and I don't always understand. The teacher doesn't use many physical examples; instead, it is mostly writing on the board and lecturing. I struggle with that.

Middle school was more laid back. We had games and activities. It seemed we had more time to learn things. But in high school, class time is only lectures and reading. I can't understand it as well. It's really tedious and boring. I prefer seeing physical demonstrations. I don't like being limited to lectures and notes, and so I am looking forward to attending a deaf school next year. I think I've had my fill of mainstreaming in hearing schools.

If I don't understand something, I'll ask the interpreter to help explain things. Like the teacher hands out the homework, and if I don't understand the written directions on the homework, I ask the interpreter, and she explains it. That way I know which part of the book to use to find the answers. If I don't understand, then I don't ask the teacher; I'll ask the interpreter.

Sam

I like going to a hearing school. I feel I have gotten a good education there. And, I've learned how to live in the hearing culture.

The experience of receiving an interpreted education seems to be significantly different from the experience of receiving a direct education. Zack's frustration with the pace of interpreting suggests a negative impact on his ability to finish his work on time. Not only does he miss recess, but he also feels singled out, which increases his feelings of embarrassment. Zack experiences "exposure embarrassment," a feeling that comes when children are aware that they have become the object of other peoples' attention. For Zack, the pain of embarrassment is constant while in the hearing classroom. In fact, the themes of embarrassment, feeling different, and feeling alienated are strong throughout Zack's interview.

Kyle emphasized another frustration of trying to learn through an interpreter. He explains that he didn't like looking between the interpreter and the "other stuff happening in the classroom." Other students also voiced this frustration, noting a desire on their part to read the teacher's expression and body language, while having access to the message. Jasmine also understands this frustration and declares that direct instruction is better because "if you have questions you can ask and get immediate responses."

Jasmine and Julie both commented that the way deaf students learn is not conducive to the way hearing students are taught. Jasmine speaks of the need for deaf students to see, touch, and manipulate things before writing about them. Without this support, she feels her only alternative is to copy from someone else or to fail. Julie also insists that deaf students are more visual learners and benefit from visual demonstrations, rather than lectures and notes. She directly links her declining success in the classroom between middle school and high school to the change in teaching methods—from visual and tactile learning to lectures and copying notes.

Several of the students mentioned they had difficulty with written instructions. Julie confesses that she does not understand the homework, which is often based on written paragraphs. Kyle and Tyler also mentioned not understanding directions. In order to appropriately accommodate deaf students, the deaf education teachers need to be active in adapting homework, tests, and projects to make them accessible to the deaf student. Tyler acknowledged this need for a strong deaf education teacher, as well.

When asked "Who do you ask when you don't understand?" some deaf students explained that they turn to the interpreter to find out what to do, but if the interpreter does not know, they might ask the teacher. Perhaps their reluctance to ask the teacher stems from their embarrassment at having a low reading level and not understanding. However, it may also reflect their view of the interpreter as the intermediary between them and the hearing world.

Again, there seems to be a great divide between the perspective of the signing deaf students and the speaking deaf students. Overall, the speaking deaf students feel more confident in their education. Perhaps because they do not rely solely on their interpreter, they are able to gain more direct information from the teacher. Sam explained that the benefit went beyond getting a good education to learning how to live in the hearing culture. She is confident in her ability to succeed in this environment and feels she is able to glean valuable skills for future use in interacting with hearing people.

Does an interpreter provide full access?

The question of "What is interpreted?" was often initially answered by a list of subjects—math, science, and art. But when I asked more probing questions, the students began to think deeper about their daily experiences in school. They discussed their awareness of conversations and sounds that occur in their environment, most of which they can not access.

Zack
She tells me what the teacher says . . . that's all. And, she tells me what to do.

Leslie
I have an interpreter in school. She interprets when I'm a little confused. Sometimes she is not there for my rotations—you know, my nine-week classes—or like gym. She uses sign. She used to use C-Print [a speech to text technology system developed at NTID], but she doesn't use it anymore.

Julie
Sometimes my friend interprets things that are going on in the classroom. The interpreter interprets conversations, sounds in the hallways, conversations between the teacher and other students. If we are walking down the hallway and I see friends, we communicate directly, so she doesn't need to interpret that, but if somebody really wants to talk with me, then she'll interpret.

Ashley
Some interpreters only focus on what the teacher says, while others with more skill let me know about the conversations around me and environmental sounds, like noises in the hallway. As long as she interprets clearly what the teacher says, I'm all right.

Schools are filled with sounds and conversations. The direct instruction of the teacher may represent only a fragment of the auditory imput from the school. What gets interpreted? What gets left out? These are important questions, and the answers vary from school to school, interpreter to interpreter.

Julie's comments give us a glimpse of the magnitude of the inter preter's role in attempting to provide full access for the deaf student. Her interpreter provided interpretation for everything happening in the classroom, as well as "conversations, sounds in the hallways, and conversations between the teacher and other students." Ashley, though, resisted the idea of using an interpreter in the hall with her. She emphasized only a need for the interpreter to provide a clear interpretation of the teacher's message. Leslie and Sam do not use an interpreter to the same extent as the other deaf students interviewed, but they did voice a need to have an interpreter available to clarify information when needed.

The needs and desires of this group of deaf students vary. While some want access to voices in the hall and environmental sounds, others only need the support of an interpretation of the teacher's voice. The responses indicate that a delicate balance exists between wanting access to the auditory environment and the possible social stigma of being followed around by an adult. The next section directly focuses on this second issue.

How does it feel to have an adult follow you around?

When asked about the availability of interaction and sounds outside of the classroom, some students shared the dilemma of choosing between access and having an adult follow them throughout the school.

Zack
I feel embarrassed [having an adult follow me through the school]. I like having natural direct communication without an interpreter.

Jasmine
I feel like I'm mentally retarded, walking around with your own adult. I feel stupid and embarrassed. But I put up with it.

Julie
That's fine. I don't mind. She's not with me *all* the time; sometimes she'll say she's going to check her messages and meet me in class, and I tell her that's fine. Or maybe in art class we are just working on our projects, so I don't really even need her to interpret at all for that class period.

Patrick
I wouldn't want her following me through the halls, or anything. But it is OK [to have her] in class.

Ashley
The interpreters generally don't follow me around the building all day long, and if they did, it would drive me crazy. I would feel like a little kid.

Some students are embarrassed by the idea of being connected to an adult in the school. They desperately want to be independent like the other kids, and yet they need adults to have access to their environment. Zack and Jasmine both connected their attachment to an interpreter with deep feelings of embarrassment. This embarrassment is also indicative of feeling alienated and different.

Other deaf students seem content with their current arrangement—a balance between independence and accessibility. Ashley explained that her interpreter does not stay with her outside of the classroom. However, this suggests that she does not have full access to the conversations and sounds occurring in those environments. Julie's comments indicate that she doesn't mind either way, but she had previously mentioned that her interpreter looks like a student, and therefore blends into the crowd. Interestingly, this might refer back to the extension theory. If your interpreter is capable of blending into your social circle, then you might not mind having her around. But if your interpreter stands out from the crowd, it could be more embarrassing.

By choosing independence over access, students reveal the depth of their need to feel independent. However, it is difficult to know whether this need for separation is based on their desire to be independent or on the social constraints imposed by their interpreter. Regardless, many deaf students freely give up access to the voices in the hall to walk alone.

What happens when your interpreter is sick or not at school?

When asked to share their experiences with substitute interpreters, several students moaned. One student even grabbed his hair and pretended to be pulling it out, in a "Yikes!" kind of pose.

Zack
[If the interpreter was sick,] I'd have other interpreters, but they were slow, not like natural signing from Deaf people. I just prefer having a deaf teacher.

Kyle
Sometimes I'd have a substitute interpreter . . . they were good, too. Some were better than others. Some interpreters would miss information.

Kaitlyn
My normal interpreter is good. But the sub is lousy. She makes me look stupid.

Leslie
When my interpreter is absent, I really don't like subs. They just don't know what to do. So, I tell my interpreter that I don't want a sub. I am better off by myself.
    One horror story: I have different schedules for every day, and I guess someone gave the sub the wrong schedule. So, she kept going to the wrong places. I kept

getting embarrassed. The sub always wanted to sit next to me, but I was sitting around my friends. I didn't really like that. They think that I *really* need their help, but I don't need it. So, I'm better off by myself.

Julie

I hate it when I have substitute interpreters. They don't read my communication very well, and I don't always understand their signs. I hate having a substitute interpreter because it just becomes a struggle.

For example, a sub interpreter might not understand some of the signs I was using, but they were regular ASL signs. I have to stop and explain each time and it gets really frustrating. Sometimes they don't understand or they just say things that don't mean the same thing that I meant and that causes problems. I've had many bad experiences with subs.

One example was last year in middle school, in art class. I had a substitute interpreter who really was not skilled enough to work. I'd had her sub for me before, so I already knew that I was likely to have problems. She interpreted the instructions from the teacher, which was fine. So I started working and the interpreter told me that I was doing it wrong and then she started doing it for me to show me how! I couldn't believe it! I told her "It's not your art project, its mine!" I started to erase what she had done and the interpreter got mad at *me*!! When the deaf education teacher found out, she really gave it to the interpreter and told her to get out and not to accept any substitute work for me again. I never really liked that interpreter, she always seemed mean to me.

If we can't get a substitute interpreter, then the deaf education teacher interprets. She's just a crazy woman, so it's a different experience and kind of fun when she does that! Actually, I'd much rather that she interpret than any other substitute.

Patrick

I usually take my classes without her.

Ashley

Sometimes I had a substitute interpreter, but usually I made it through on my own if the interpreter wasn't there. I had a regular class schedule, so I knew what to do for each class. Sometimes the class activities really required having an interpreter, and then it was hard, but at least I was there.

A disturbing trend emerged in the comments of the deaf students. The quality of interpreting and professionalism of the substitute interpreters was so poor that several deaf students would rather not have an interpreter for the day than to have a substitute. Kyle's comments reflected a concern that unqualified interpreters may miss information presented to the class, while Zack pointed out that they were slow. Julie mentioned her frustration when the substitute interpreter did not understand her signs and incorrectly voiced her comments to the class. Ashley either chose not to have an interpreter or was not provided with one. In all cases, the consequences have an ominous impact on the academic achievement of deaf students. Having full access to classroom instruction is a primary prerequuisite to the deaf students' ability to learn.

The behavior of substitute interpreters also had a negative impact on the perceived social status of the deaf students. Julie and Leslie each related a personal social crisis that occurred because the substitute interpreter's behavior embarrassed them—another possible indicator of the interpreter extension theory. Julie's horror story recounted the substitute interpreter's attempt to micromanage Julie's activities in class. Leslie's horror story was a result of inappropriate support in that someone gave the interpreter the incorrect schedule. In Leslie's experience, the real tragedy went beyond the substitute's pattern of appearing in the wrong place at the wrong time. The substitute also did not understand Leslie's social habits in the classroom or her typical method of using the interpreter for clarification purposes. In both Julie's and Leslie's stories, perceived social harm occurred because the substitutes were not aware of the students' social needs in the classroom. In all, it is clear that most deaf students have a negative opinion of substitute interpreters.

Building Relationships in a Hearing School

Regular Education Teachers

How do you feel about your regular ed. teachers?

When asked about their opinions of the regular education teachers,* students initially answered with "they are nice" remarks. However, in answering the probing questions, they began to delve into deeper issues of perceived inferiority and lack of communication.

---

* NOTE: During the interviews, deaf students often referred to the regular education teachers as the "hearing teacher." They referred to the deaf education teacher as their "deaf teacher." This is reflective of the teachers ability/inability to sign, rather than their hearing status.

Zack

Only once in a while [I communicated with the hearing teachers]. With deaf teachers, communication is no problem. If you need help, you just ask them and they tell you what something means. The hearing teachers had to ask the interpreter. It was hard, and sometimes I still didn't understand.

Kyle

The hearing teachers tried to communicate with me; sometimes they talked and used a microphone system, but it was still really hard to hear and understand anything. It was just hard because they would try to talk to me, but it was really hard to understand them. If I didn't understand the work we were doing, like if I didn't understand the directions, I'd sometimes ask the interpreter, and if the interpreter didn't know what to do then I'd ask the teacher.

Leslie

I think they know that I am deaf, but they know that I can do everything everyone else can do. They don't put me below anyone else, which I like.

Patrick

Usually funny ones are the best. I have this one teacher who is really boring. He has absolutely no personality, and he just has a deadpan face and talks on and on and on! My interpreter is really funny. She keeps me entertained.

Jasmine

How about the hearing teachers?
I don't care about the teachers.

Did you communicate with your hearing teachers?
Interpreters, but not me.

Did the hearing teachers try to communicate with you?
[It went] over my head . . . I'm deaf. Sometimes they use the wrong signs.

Did the hearing teachers consider you the same as the hearing kids?
No. They are like, "I'm trying to learn how to talk with you." No, they sign the wrong way. Communication is much more natural with other deaf people. I mean, if you know how to communicate, then go ahead, but do it the right way. But from what I see, I don't have a good reason to stop and talk.

How do you communicate with your hearing teachers?

Julie

I use natural, cultural gestures like WHATEVER and LOSER and basic stuff. They don't really want to learn sign language, just a few funny things, that's all they want to learn. The only real communication happens when the interpreter is there. Sometimes I get into class before the interpreter does, and if the teacher tries to talk to me I just point to my ears, indicating that I'm deaf. I smile and I just wait until the interpreter comes . . . or sometimes my best friend will interpret for me.

Are you being taught the same as hearing kids?
It's the same. They ask me questions just like everyone else. But I don't answer if I don't feel like it . . . because I don't have to. But if I say something, then the interpreter puts it into spoken English and that's fine.

Do you start conversations with the teacher?
Not often. I talk with the math teacher, who's nice. We'll talk about math, and sometimes we joke back and forth a bit.

Ashley
Some of my hearing teachers learned some signs. Either they were really interested or maybe they had deaf students before. Some thought it was fun to learn about different cultures and how people interact as compared to hearing interaction. Other teachers didn't care to learn anything.

As for communication with the teachers, some were flexible and willing to communicate with me directly, sometimes by writing notes. Other teachers only communicated with me when the interpreter was present. I think they considered me just as much their student as everyone else in the class with the understanding that I needed some accommodation to get the information visually. Otherwise I was just another student in the classroom. I might ask questions during class or sometimes when class was finished.

Sam
Do you feel the teachers treat you as an equal to the hearing students?
No, that is probably the one bad thing. My mom keeps telling the teachers that I am equal and to not treat me as less capable, but the teachers still do. Sometimes I'm just plain lazy, and I don't work as hard as I should. My teachers let me slide by.

⟫◆⟪

When discussing the hearing teachers, the deaf students suggest that some teachers seemed interested in learning about their culture and their language. At the same time, others were not. They seemed to feel a deeper connection with the teachers who did learn at least a few signs. Julie suggested that her teachers just wanted to learn a few funny signs, to use in joking around. Perhaps for those teachers, this represents a desire to make the student feel more accepted and comfortable in the classroom. However, Julie did not perceive it as a sincere interest in her culture. Jasmine also recognized a lack of sincerity from the teachers and seemed frustrated that even when they did learn some signs, they did not use them correctly.

Another theme that emerged from the student interviews was the lack of interaction between the hearing teacher and the deaf student. Zack and Jasmine both suggested that the teacher talked with the interpreter, not them. They did not see the interpreter as a funnel through which a conversation took place between them and the hearing teacher. Instead, they viewed this phenomenon as two mini conversations: one between themselves and the interpreter, and the other between the interpreter and the hearing teacher. Zack and Jasmine both compared their experiences in public school with their current deaf school setting. They prefer having direct communication with the teacher of the deaf because they are able ask questions and receive clarification directly.

Some of the deaf students indicated that teachers may use a variety of strategies to communicate with them. Ashley explained that some of her teachers were very flexible and would write notes to communicate, while others tried to communicate directly. Kyle explained how his teachers used the FM system, although he did not find this helpful.

Interestingly, Patrick noted his teacher's lack of variety in communication strategies. But he seemed relieved that his interpreter livened up the lecture with her own funny insertions. Obviously, this practice of insertion is highly controversial, in that some view the role of an interpreter as being a communication facilitator only. From a conservative perspective, equality is the goal—if the hearing students are sitting through a boring lecture, then the deaf student must do the same. Patrick, however, is grateful for the diversion.

Several students expressed their frustration at not understanding the teacher, even when the message had been interpreted. They did not provide specific examples, which makes it nearly impossible to identify the source of this difficulty. Some possible reasons are poor placement, interpreter error, lack of accommodations, and lack of teacher clarity or cultural competency. However, the very process of interpreting in the education system introduces a new set of junctures where communication breakdown might occur.

Another point raised by some of the students was whether or not the teacher accepted them as equals to the hearing students. Julie felt that she was asked questions in class just like the other students. Ashley mentioned that she felt comfortable asking questions in class. Leslie also indicated a strong sense of being accepted as an equal. However, both Julie and Sam revealed that their teachers exhibited lower expectations of them. While Sam's mother unsuccessfully fought this notion, Julie seemed to use it to her advantage. Although the teacher did ask her questions, Julie did not always answer because she felt she didn't "have to." Interestingly, her reply reveals a sense of exceptionality. Curiously, some deaf students learn to spin the peculiarities of being different to serve them in a manner that they feel is quite favorable.

Communicating With Hearing Peers

How do deaf students communicate with the hearing students in school? During each interview, the topic of communicating with hearing peers was addressed. While some deaf students focused on the hearing students' ability to sign to them, other deaf students focused on their own frustrations in the communication process.

Did any of the hearing kids sign?

Zack
Not really, only so-so.

Kyle
Some of the hearing kids learned how to sign a little. Some didn't learn any signs at all. I prefer being at the deaf school because we communicate a lot with each other. The hearing kids couldn't sign well, and it was hard to communicate at the hearing school.

Leslie
I've always used my voice to talk to the other kids, even when I was little. But I can sign [to the deaf students], too!

How do you communicate with the hearing kids?

Zack
I can't understand them. They speak and I don't understand them. I can't talk. . . .
I sign, so they don't understand me. It's hard to communicate. If girls or boys try to talk to me, I don't understand them, I feel stuck not understanding them, and that's why I'm embarrassed.

Julie

First I start by teaching them fingerspelling, and then basic signs, and we just keep going until they are as fluent as they can be. For my best friend, it took her two years, maybe two and a half years, for her to get really fluent in ASL. I met her in sixth grade, and she was interested in learning, so she just kept at it, asking me to teach her, and she talked with me a lot, so we became friends—best friends—and we still are.

But now we have arguments and disagreements. She's the one who starts the fights. I put up with her because she's the only one I can communicate with, and it is so hard to teach other people to communicate. I mean, I'm happy to help people learn how to communicate with me, but it takes so long until they get fluent. It takes a lot of effort, and I'm a bit tired of working so hard just to have friends I can talk with.

Patrick

I feel good. I have so many friends. We are always doing fun things together. They know some signs, but mostly they just gesture. I hang out with them sometimes on the weekends. We are always talking on IM when we are not at school. They are pretty cool.

Ashley

Some of my classmates were interested in learning some signs, and I would teach them a few . . . not more than for some basic communication. We didn't really write much . . . except maybe to pass notes to each other during class, but that's just normal.

There's only about two or three people who sign in the school . . . either they have deaf family members or they grew up with a deaf friend. There's not too many who sign, so mostly I use my voice and talk with people at school.

Sam

Many people have learned ASL at my school, so I have a lot of people that I can talk to—at least to some degree. My school offers ASL 1, ASL 2, and ASL 3.

How many kids at school can sign well?

Julie

My best friend and one other . . . that's it, just two people who sign well.

What do you talk to them about?

The hearing kids tend to talk about boyfriends a lot. They go on forever about their boyfriends. We'll talk about school, about going out to do things. We talked about Easter, about Jesus and the crucifixion. We talk about the art teacher who gets mad sometimes and throws things . . . things people do that are funny and make us laugh.

In order to access the social web of student culture, deaf students must be able to communicate with their hearing peers. When communication is limited, it directly affects their ability to build quality relationships with peers. It is not surprising, therefore, to see the level of social isolation that the signing deaf students reveal. From the responses of Zack, Kyle, Ashley, and Julie, we can assume that very few hearing students learn ASL well enough to hold a conversation. Ashley and Julie named only two people in each of their schools who could sign fairly well.

Zack talked about his embarrassment and the awkwardness he felt when trying to communicate with hearing students. By feeling embarrassed and "stuck," Zack indicated that he felt responsible for the communication barrier. It would be interesting to know if the hearing student felt equally uncomfortable. Zack believed a communication breakdown could occur at any moment, and this gave him a constant feeling of stress and nervousness. Thus, the moment of communication breakdown increases the deaf student's feelings of being isolated and of feeling different.

Julie gives us a glimpse of the heavy burden of time and patience necessary in teaching someone to sign. She explains that she created a friend by first finding a girl who was interested in learning ASL. She daily taught the girl how to communicate through sign language and, two years later, her friend finally had become fluent. But the joy of having a friend was somewhat diminished by the fact that the friendship was growing sour. When the friend engaged in unbecoming behavior, Julie felt stuck with her because she was the only one with whom she could communicate. Interestingly, Julie's choice of a friend was not based on common interests or mutual respect. Instead, it was based on who was willing to learn sign language, therefore becoming very limiting. Also, Julie felt her motivation to teach someone else the language was withering because of the great time commitment she had already invested in the first friend. For the signing deaf students, this severe limitation in building friendships is most likely an indicator of an accompanying severe limitation in social experiences.

Again, the speaking deaf students seemed to experience greater satisfaction in this area. Leslie noted that she could communicate with the hearing students through voice, and the deaf students through sign. She seemed particularly pleased that she was able to communicate bilingually with each group in their preferred method, and therefore perhaps she had a greater range of peer relationships than many others. Patrick seemed to fully enjoy his peer relationships. He also mentioned that they were able to use Instant Messenger in the evenings to communicate. Perhaps he felt that this was a forum in which he could communicate on more even ground. Though he does not specifically mention how he communicates with his friends, it is assumed that he verbally speaks to communicate, since he later states that his friends only know a few signs and mostly gesture.

Sam, however, seemed more satisfied with the communication she had among her peers. Not only is she able to communicate to a great extent through voice, but she also has the advantage of attending a high school that teaches ASL as a foreign language. Although she indicated that the signing level of these students did not reach the fluent level, she did feel that this greatly increased the number of people with whom she could interact. In all, it is important to note that every speaking deaf student reported some positive feelings about their relationships with hearing students.

Being Friends With Hearing Peers

What is it like to be friends with the hearing students?

This is a question that only deaf students can answer. For many of them, it took a moment of thinking to be able to express their deeply held emotions of trying to be friends with someone who doesn't share their language.

Tyler
> When I meet a deaf student, they want to stay in a small group. The deaf kids only want to sit and socialize only with other deaf kids. At deaf schools everyone signs; this is easier. If the deaf kids only sign in a hearing school, the hearing kids don't talk to us.

Jasmine
> Well, it seemed I had a lot of friends in hearing school who were my age. But they're not my friends if they try to take advantage of deaf people. They just want to learn sign language to look cool. If they really like deaf people, then we can be friends. I have two friends who don't like hearing people, just deaf people, like me.

Julie
> Sometimes I just give up. I've spent all these years in mainstreamed schools. I don't have the experience of a deaf school and having a wide choice of people to be

friends with. My friends had no other knowledge about deaf people besides me, so they had to learn about deafness and deaf people. At deaf camp, however, everyone is either deaf or knows about deafness, so it's not an issue—communication is immediate with everyone, so it's not a problem. But I don't have that option at the hearing school, so I just have to put up with it.

Sure [the hearing kids] get together with friends. I mean best friends will go and do things together. And I'll do some things with my friend, too. But her parents are strict, so we have to have permission each time, so I can't just go and get together with friends any time I want to.

Zack

I just played with one deaf friend, Nick. That's all. My friends before were . . . David and Nick. David was hearing and Nick was deaf. Usually David just talked and Nick interpreted for me.

Nick can talk, he's hard of hearing. But I'm not hard of hearing, I'm deaf. If Nick was sick, David would still try to talk to me, but I couldn't understand him. That's why I felt stuck.

Ashley

I'm the kind of person who makes friends easily so it's not too hard for me to have hearing friends.

━━◈◆◈━━

Signing deaf students who have grown up in hearing schools do not demonstrate a full understanding of the relationship-building process that usually results in someone becoming a friend. Though they identified a particular person as their friend, they later confessed that they had never had a conversation with this person—they only waved to each other in the hall. Ashley felt that she made friends quite easily at school but later she explained that her friends didn't sign, and they only communicated on a minimal level.

The strain of trying to build friendships without communication is often reflected in the frustrating tone of the comments. Here, again, a great divide exists between the signing deaf students and the speaking deaf students. It is clear from Zack's response that young children do not have the coping mechanisms to change the manner in which they communicate. Zack's reflection was from early elementary school, where children may not easily be able to write their thoughts, and deaf children may be even less capable of reading and understanding written communication. Zack's commentary shows the essential arrangement of the middle person, a hard of hearing child who bridges the gap. Without this child's involvement, the communication and the friendship comes completely to a halt. Zack says that *he* feels stuck when the communication breaks down due to the lack of shared language access. He also mentions that his hard of hearing friend interprets for him while his hearing friend does most of the talking. This kind of unequal relationship may be related to "caretaker" talk (Ramsey, 1997).

Jasmine relates her feeling of being used as a tool to make the other students look cool. Her first comment that "it seemed I had lots of friends" is quickly followed by a counter-argument that indicates that perhaps they were not really her friends. Interestingly, she seems to have created her own litmus test of friendship—if you really like deaf people, and not hearing people, you can be her friend.

Julie's comments focus on the lack of choices for friendship. While hearing students have a school full of choices for friendships, she is limited to the two people who have actually learned enough to communicate directly with her. Though the normal social experiences of teenagers often lead to changes in friends, Julie is unable to let go of a more painful relationship, because she doesn't have anyone else from which to choose. Julie also feels the pressure of being the only deaf representative to the school, yet, she has assumed sole responsibility for teaching others about deaf culture.

The students with more speech and lipreading ability have more normal friendship relationships. They spend time outside of school with their friends and often feel included in conversations. But Tyler also shares how he sometimes feels torn between being friends with the deaf students and the hearing students. His insightful comment reveals the core of the problem: "If the deaf students only sign, the hearing kids won't talk to us." Interestingly, he doesn't put the pressure on the hearing kids to learn sign language, but instead he places the responsibility for bridging the gap onto the deaf students. This observation is unusual because the hearing kids are capable of learning sign language, but the deaf students may not have the ability to learn to speak. At the end of his quote, Tyler clearly identifies himself as being one of the deaf students. From the speaking deaf student's perspective, Tyler's comments reveal the mediator role that speaking deaf students may adopt between the two groups. This notion is supported in the perception of the signing deaf student found in Zack's quote: "Usually David just talked and Nick interpreted for me."

Overall, it seems that the signing deaf students have a deeper struggle in building friendships with hearing peers. It also is likely that speaking deaf students in schools with both hearing peers and signing deaf peers tend to serve as communication mediators between the two groups. In this study, the speaking deaf students with greater speaking ability reported feelings of greater acceptance by their hearing peers.

Improving Integrated Education

Some of the students offered suggestions on how schools could improve the success of deaf students.

Leslie

Well, my mom she goes to school in fall to arrange for my teachers, and who I will get. My sister graduated this year, so she had the teachers that I am going to have. So, my mom knows which teachers are good and bad. So, my mom goes in early, before school starts, and helps decide which teachers I will have. They also arrange my schedule so that my interpreter can come in the morning and then go home—because she has kids, too.

Julie

My teacher and interpreter work well together, and the interpreter sometimes helps me to understand concepts better when we are in the resource room and she's not even technically interpreting. It's really an overall comfort that we have with each other, all three of us. They know who I am, my family, and I know about them, too. If we didn't know each other that well, then people might get angry, but we are flexible and cooperate with each other. They help me better understand concepts with real-life examples. So I really appreciate that closeness that we share.

[The deaf education teacher and interpreter] set up fun activities for my friends. For example, I had a friend on the soccer team who wanted to learn more signs and communicate with me. So we invited her to come to the resource room during class time and watch a video. She was thrilled with the idea of being able to skip a class, and that built her motivation to learn more sign and communicate with me even better. So we have hearing students in the room to eat lunches, watch videos with popcorn, or just to have conversations. The teacher sets up these activities, and it helps motivate people to learn better how to communicate with me, so that helps a lot.

Also, my school allows my deaf education teacher to specifically choose my teachers for the next school year. She chooses teachers that she knows will be flexible and welcoming to me. She also works with the school to get a few friends who have learned sign language in my classes. That way, I have other people to talk to other than just my interpreter. It works out really well when we are assigned to group projects. My signing friends can work with me, which means I can feel more a part of the project because I can communicate directly with them. My teacher has been putting us in the same classes for several years, so they are finally getting more fluent at signing.

Ashley

There are several problems that could be improved upon to make schools better for deaf kids. One is that the hearing classrooms have the social interaction, but they are separated from the resource rooms and the hearing support teacher. I think this causes the deaf kid to be at a lower and lower level than the hearing kids as each year passes. It would also really help if the hearing students had sign language classes. They never had sign language classes for the hearing kids at my school.

Sam

Well, my school offers ASL as a foreign language. Even though those students aren't really skilled, at least it gives me some choices in who I can talk to.

———◆———

In giving advice for how schools could better meet the needs of deaf students, Ashley seems to acknowledge that the implied distance between the hearing classroom and the support of the resource room and teacher has a direct impact on the way students are viewed by their hearing peers. She also recognizes that the value of sign classes may broaden her social experiences. This seems to be confirmed in Sam's comments that attending a school where ASL is taught is definitely helpful, although the students are not fluent.

Leslie encouraged schools to give parents and students the power to choose teachers who were especially adaptive and supportive of deaf students. She attributes much of her success to her mom's ability to hand select her teachers. Julie also attributes her success to having her teacher choose flexible and welcoming teachers. Sadly, this indicates that not all teachers are welcoming and flexible in meeting the needs of deaf students.

Julie moves beyond the importance of choosing flexible teachers and insists that deaf education teachers need to be involved in choosing hearing peers for the class. Julie's teacher has found a few hearing students who are interested in learning sign language and has had them placed in Julie's classes. This represents a flexible school policy of empowering the deaf education teacher to influence the scheduling of other students. It is also assumed that these class placements were first determined to be mutually beneficial for the hearing students.

Julie recognizes the importance of a positive relationship between herself, the interpreter, and the teacher of the deaf. She finds this closeness to be an important element of her success. The fact that they know her family gives her an overall sense of comfort and helps her to feel valued and welcomed in the school environment. Perhaps it is the feeling of having allies that provides support and encouragement to her in being the only deaf high school student. She feels that they want her to succeed and will do whatever it takes to help her understand the material.

Julie's deaf education teacher and interpreter have an exceptional focus on supporting Julie's social learning needs. They have found innovative ways to increase her social circle and at the same time promote social friendships. For example, Julie describes inviting her hearing friends to lunch in the resource classroom, where they watch sign movies and eat popcorn. These activities do not "just happen" but instead are planned for and implemented by her deaf education teacher, in cooperation with the regular education school faculty. This school demonstrates much greater flexibility, cultural competency, and sensitivity to deaf students' needs than may be found in other schools.

With this in mind, it might be tempting to create an "input" type of model, believing that if teachers do these things, deaf students will no longer struggle with the big issues of language deprivation, isolation, and loneliness. However, it is important to note that even in this highly supportive environment, Julie still struggles with feeling lonely. Despite all of these positive strategies for helping her build friendships in hearing schools, she still believes that integrated environments are not the best place for deaf students. She sees the divide between cultures and languages as an uncrossable barrier to providing real success for deaf students in hearing learning environments. Later, when Julie was asked, "What would you do to make the school better for deaf kids?" she replied,

> I'm not sure you can do that. . . . Improvements for deaf kids would basically work against what the hearing kids need. I mean, you have two different cultures, two different sets of basic needs. It's good for each group to learn about the other and interact with each other, but the basic needs are in conflict.

Her answer seems to reflect a maturity of understanding—the basic needs of two cultures are in conflict in this environment.

Unexpected Findings

During the interviews, several issues surfaced that were unexpected. Though they were not within the original scope of the study, they are noteworthy in that they provide a deeper understanding of the education of deaf students in integrated environments.

Accommodating or Cheating?

Several students quietly divulged that their interpreters and/or deaf education teachers helped them to cheat. With apparent embarrassment and guilt they shared this secret and expressed a concern that they weren't learning anything. A couple of students asked me for advice in how to deal with this situation. Because this area was especially embarrassing to the student, they will be shared anonymously.

Student #1

I have tests and homework in my classes with the interpreter, and we work on those assignments in the resource room. But sometimes the deaf education teacher doesn't push me as much as she should, and she'll just answer the questions or do the work for me. Generally I'm OK in the classroom, but I feel guilty that I didn't do all the work myself. I guess we do this mostly in math because I really don't like that class at all, so it's just too easy for her to do it rather than explain it to me well enough for me to do it. Some of the teachers are flexible, and they are OK about making these kinds of adjustments, but I still don't feel it is the right way to do it. It's not like I'm copying other people's work, but a lot of the time I am copying things out of the book to answer questions. It's not really good.

Student #2

My interpreter and deaf education teacher seem to do more spoon-feeding, like I'm a baby. They take care of tests and make it easy to pass tests. I was supposed to have math in the fall, and I never learned math; they just passed me anyway. They never really taught me how to do math. I don't have homework or really have to learn anything. My teacher does all my homework for me. I never have to.

Student #3

[My deaf ed. teacher] is nice, but I feel I am behind. . . . The deaf education teacher lets me be lazy with my English, reading, and writing. I feel that we have skipped a lot of instruction this year. We just sit around and chat. It's been six months; I don't feel like I'm doing any work in those areas, and I am getting concerned that I might get low grades next year because I'm not learning as much as I should.

Sometimes my deaf ed. teacher sets up fun outings and activities for the two of us to do together. Actually, I think one reason the deaf education teacher does this is that she's just lazy and doesn't want to teach me every day. I don't think I'm getting the education I should be getting.

Student #4

I never hear the morning announcements. My interpreter is supposed to be at school to tutor me when I arrive. But she knows no one will notice, so she shows up 45 minutes late every morning. So, I just sit in the resource room by myself and do my homework by myself. When she does get there, she just tells me the answers—to kind of make up for being late. She says, "If I tell you the answers, you don't tell anyone that I show up to school 45 minutes late every morning." But no one is there to interpret the morning announcements. Recently, I noticed a bunch of girls out on the field playing girls' softball. I wished I would have known about it. I would have joined the team. My interpreter also shows up late for some of my classes. She is too busy talking with other teachers. So, I'm stuck in class without knowing what my teacher is saying.

Student #5

My deaf ed. teacher never shows up at the right time. And at least once a week, she says she's sick and goes home at lunch. I spend a lot of time sitting in the resource room, not getting what I'm supposed to get. It's a waste of my time. It's like they don't think my education is important. Even the speech teacher doesn't show up half the time, and when she does show up, she sits around and chats with the teacher and interpreter during my speech time. I finally just get started on speech, when it is over. It is a total waste of my time. I haven't really told anyone about all this, but it's just making me angry.

⟫⟫◆⟪⟪

When teachers and interpreters work in isolation, it may have a significant effect on their work ethic. It is as though they say, "If no one is watching, no one will notice I'm slacking." But someone is watching; and it is the deaf student. Clearly, the deaf students perceive the teacher and interpreter's waning work ethic to be a direct affront to their education. When teachers, interpreters, and therapists do not follow through with their commitments, they are quietly indicating to the deaf student that their education is of less importance. This unprofessional behavior of placing priority on their own socialization needs over the student's education has clearly angered some deaf students. Though these professionals may feel they have only committed slight misconduct, collectively they represent the heavy, oppressive nature of low expectations, as well as producing a serious blow to the education of deaf students.

Curiously, several students were frustrated with the level of cheating they felt takes place by their teacher and interpreter. In defense of the professionals, perhaps these measures were simply accommodations. For example, if the deaf education teacher feels an assignment is too difficult, she would have the option of working through it with the deaf student. However, the deaf student needs to be informed of the accommodations being made and clearly informed of how they will be expected to be accountable for the information. On the other hand, it does seem that teachers and interpreters may be motivated to "make the deaf student look good." If the student is doing well, then it would follow that the interpreter and the teacher must be terrific. But if the student is failing, then it may cast doubt on the abilities of the professionals who support him or her. Most disturbing is the account from student #4, who spoke of cheating as an unwritten agreement between her and the interpreter; this is dangerously close to blackmail. Considering the enormous role of the interpreter in the student's life, it is nothing less than appalling.

Comparing Educational Environments: Deaf Schools vs. Integrated Environments

Three students are experiencing their first year in a school for the deaf. Zack and Jasmine had experienced deaf schools earlier in their life, but Kyle is being exposed to this environment for the first time. Though Ashley has never experienced education at a deaf school, she bases her opinions on what she has heard and seen from others in deaf schools.

Kyle
My deaf school is better because the communication is so much easier

Zack
When I was nine I moved to a school for the deaf. It's easy to communicate and get along with everyone there, so age nine and ten have been good. Its easy to communicate; I don't feel embarrassed. It's a lot better.

I was quiet [in the hearing school]. At the hearing school, I might say something once in a while, but I was mostly pretty quiet. At [the deaf school], we talk all the time, in the after school program, in the classroom, at recess. There's a lot of communication. With hearing kids it was different, always speaking, communication wasn't very interesting. At the deaf school everyone communicates all the time, and I have many friends there. So the deaf school is better.

Do you feel you learned a lot in hearing school?

No . . . I didn't like it when people talked and I didn't understand them. At my deaf school it is easy to talk to anyone any time I talk with boys and girls. We talk outside, at recess, in the after-school program. People can get in different groups to talk. I spent a lot of time at the hearing school just waiting and bored, but at my deaf school, I can talk with anyone. It's better with deaf people. I can understand better and succeed. I'm getting As and Bs, maybe a C, but lots of As at the deaf school.

Jasmine

For ninth grade, I attended a school for the deaf, and there are many deaf people there and it is very easy to communicate and socialize with everyone. They don't have patience for the attitude that deaf people are mentally lower than hearing people. There, everyone is equal. So with easy communication I realized that I'm not dumb and I can succeed in school. Now I know I can do things for myself. Now I'm finally learning math and I'm catching up to algebra. I feel that I am also catching up in English. I'm up to a sixth-grade reading level now. Since being there I feel it is much better than being at the hearing school.

It's different at the hearing school; it is hard to have friends and boyfriends because they aren't like me to start with; I have to teach them. At the deaf school there are many people like me, so it is easy to find friends and boyfriends. I like the deaf school because I see people who share my culture and subgroups who share my values. At the hearing school, communication is more restricted and formal. At the deaf school you can directly say what you want and get straight to the point. Whether it's in the dorm or in the classroom . . . if you want to know something you just ask. The teacher will give an example and encourage you. At the hearing school I would just sit and go through classes. They would just talk, and if you didn't understand, then it was too bad for you; plus, there were no social opportunities after school. I look at the deaf school and feel a personal connection and identity. I just didn't get any of that at the hearing school. I prefer students like me . . . deaf.

As for college, maybe going to Gallaudet or hearing colleges I don't think it will matter, but there still needs to be some deaf students so you can still socialize. If there aren't other deaf people there, then you might feel lonely or depressed, then you can't work or think. With other deaf people around, then you feel safe and it is easy to focus, think, and succeed. You can keep busy.

Ashley

As for comparing deaf and hearing schools, that's hard because I never attended a deaf school. From what I see in the deaf community, people who went to deaf schools have stronger ties to other deaf people. The one concern I have is that it seems that deaf schools don't provide as high an education as the hearing schools do. If they were equal, then I think a deaf school is fine, but for now graduates of deaf schools have to try to catch up with the graduates of hearing schools.

Though the students were never asked to compare their educational experiences, they seemed to do so naturally again and again. Throughout their responses, strong themes emerged of the benefits of their deaf school. These themes included having a shared language, greater depth and variety in friendships, an education that matches the way they learn, and feeling like they belong. Zack is exuberant about in the ability to talk to so many different people. He also views this change in his learning environment as being integral to his change in personality—from being quiet and withdrawn to being outgoing and happy.

Both Zack and Jasmine link their newfound communication freedom with improved academic achievement. For Jasmine, the deaf school is a place where everyone is treated equal. Without the oppressive attitude of low expectations she felt in the hearing school, Jasmine believes she can finally succeed. She further associates her ability to socialize with other deaf people to her ability to "work and think." Interestingly, she believes she feels safe with other deaf people around. Perhaps this is due to a sense of having a community that is her support structure. She also believes that having access to other deaf people serves as a safeguard against loneliness and depression.

Jasmine discovered a change in herself—that of an empowered person. This realization is embedded in her poignant statement, "I realized that I'm not dumb and I can succeed in school. Now I know I can do things for myself." Her self-image has blossomed to include success.

Finally, the joy of having a shared identify is obvious from both Jasmine and Zack's responses. From Jasmine's comments, we can infer that it was difficult to find a boyfriend in the hearing school. Since boy-girl relationships are increasingly at the core of student social culture for middle school and high school students, it could be painful to be left out of this realm. Jasmine also emphasizes her need to be in a place that recognizes her culture and identity. She is happy in a place that meets her various social and academic needs.

While Ashley acknowledges that deaf people have stronger ties to the deaf community, she also expresses a common opinion—that the education at schools for the deaf do not meet the same high quality standards of regular education schools. Ashley points out the give-and-take relationship between the two options, and she chooses academic achievement over social opportunities. In contrast, Jasmine's comments counter that social experiences and academic achievement are closely intertwined and therefore lead to mutual success.

An Interpretation of Deaf Students' Collective Responses

Overall, several strong themes emerged as the deaf student participants discussed their lived experiences in hearing schools. The most basic underlying themes of their entire discourse were language deprivation and social isolation. The students emphasized again and again the importance of accessing the social side of learning. They mentioned the ability or inability to access social experiences in school in almost every topic addressed. Since a significant divergence of experiences and opinions exists between the deaf signing students and the speaking deaf students, the following analysis will treat these two groups separately.

The Signing Deaf Students

The signing deaf students expressed mostly negative feelings about their experiences in hearing schools and tended to see integrated schools as inadequate places for deaf children to learn. They specifically revealed themes of language deprivation, social isolation, inferiority, and lack of power.

Feelings of language deprivation and social isolation seemed intertwined and evident in the responses of almost all deaf signing students. They indicated a severe lack of direct interaction with others both in their environment and in relationship building. For the most part, the deaf signing students did not feel connected to their hearing teachers. They revealed that they rarely interacted with the hearing teachers and that the teachers often seemed disinterested in learning their language and their culture. They also expressed frustration at the teachers' display of low expectations toward them, as compared to their hearing peers.

The signing deaf students also had limited access to the social web of student culture in their school. Some deaf students did not have a clear understanding of the relationship-building process that is embedded in the concept *friend.* They loosely recognized individuals as their friends and later realized that they did not have a relationship with that person. Through many examples and stories, they expressed their deep struggle with loneliness and isolation, often linking these feelings to a lack of ability to learn.

The deaf students were never able to establish satisfactory communication with the hearing students, and they seemed to feel responsible for this lack of communication, which led to embarrassment and feeling different. Even some of the speaking deaf students criticized signing deaf students for not being able to communicate more effectively with the hearing students.

In some student responses, cultural isolation emerged as a theme. The feeling that their culture and language were neither understood nor valued by anyone in their environment left them feeling alienated and lonely. They felt that they were being forced to assimilate into the majority culture, and their inability to do so seemed to give them a sense of being powerless.

The theme of inferiority was also prominent in many student responses. It was embedded in the students' inward feelings of being inferior to the hearing students. It was also embedded in their experiences with teachers who seemed to have lower expectations for their learning outcomes. Inferiority was found in their experiences of being bullied and seen as less capable by their peers. It was also found when blame was laid on the signing deaf students for being unable to communicate with hearing peers. Finally, inferiority was recognized by some students in the hearing world's insistence that they become more like hearing people and disregard deaf language and culture.

A theme of powerlessness seemed to surface in the diminished control deaf students had in language interaction. While hearing students are able to communicate directly with everyone in their environment, deaf students must depend heavily on interpreters who voice for them. This lack of power also carried over to their inability to choose friends. Often deaf students do not have the luxury of choosing their friends in the same manner hearing students do. Instead, they are often limited to the hearing students who are interested in learning sign language.

Speaking Deaf Students

Overall, the speaking deaf students tended to express mostly positive feelings about their school environment. They did not seem to experience the same level of social isolation that was experienced by the deaf signing students. Though the speaking deaf students seemed to find more satisfaction in the social and academic areas of school, they still experienced frustrations that led to feelings of loneliness and isolation. However, even the speaking deaf students revealed that they experience frustration due to the communication barrier. Though it may not be as intense as it is for their deaf signing counterparts, they still described moments when they did not understand their teachers and hearing peers—leading them to feelings of loneliness and of being different. They also revealed their frustration in being thought of by peers and teachers as being less capable. It seemed this indicator of inferiority was felt by even the deaf students with strong speech and hearing skills.

The speaking deaf students did seem to more easily access their education through the combined use of an interpreter and their own limited abilities to hear and speak. They seemed to recognize that these limited abilities to hear and speak greatly increased their capacity to form relationships with hearing peers. And insightfully, they noticed the limitations that the inability to speak imposed on their signing deaf student counterparts.

Interestingly, the responses of the speaking deaf students seemed to indicate that they may play the role of an intermediary between their signing deaf and hearing friends. However, they also may feel torn between the two, while ultimately identifying themselves with the deaf students. Several speaking deaf students revealed a desire to know more about deaf culture and to identify more closely with deaf people.

Combined Perspectives on the Complexities of an Interpreted Education

Another string of themes emerged when the deaf students discussed their experiences in receiving an interpreted education. These themes focused around the complexities of receiving an interpreted education, their view of the interpreter as an extension of themselves, their desire for the interpreter to be a friend or ally, and their deep frustrations with substitute interpreters.

An interpreted education seems to be significantly different from the experience of receiving a direct education. In learning through an interpreter, students expressed several frustrations, such as the slowness of the interpreter, having to look back and forth between the interpreter and teacher, not being taught in a way that stimulates visual and tactile learning, and not understanding the teacher.

When asked "What makes someone a *good* interpreter?" deaf students seemed to emphasize the social and physical attributes of the interpreter, rather than skill. Although a couple of students did mention the need for highly skilled interpreters, most students focused on social and physical attributes instead. It seemed that this emphasis reinforced the level to which the deaf student sees the interpreter as an extension of himself/herself in the social setting. This theory has been labeled the *extension theory* in this study to further clarify the deaf students' relationship with their interpreter. When asked to describe the perfect interpreter, students chose attributes that they themselves had. For example, most deaf students preferred young and fun interpreters who were of the same sex as the student. The older students also wanted youthful interpreters who could blend in and look like a student. Some students had very distinct opinions about what kind of clothes their interpreter should wear, as well as their age and body type.

Another indicator of the extension theory is in the students' feelings of being embarrassed by their interpreters' or substitute interpreters' clothes or actions. It seemed clear that signing deaf students felt that the level to which their interpreter was accepted by their hearing peers was the level to which they would also be accepted. From this perspective, an interpreter who was seen as unattractive or unapproachable by hearing students would severely limit their social interactions with the deaf student. Therefore, deaf students may develop very strong opinions about the mannerisms, personality, and clothes of their interpreter because they feel these factors directly reflect on their own social acceptance at school.

Deaf students also seem to balance language access and the social stigma of having an adult following them around. One deaf student, with a very young interpreter, seemed to enjoy hanging out with her interpreter in the halls because she blended in with the students. Other students, with interpreters who may not have blended into the social scene in the hall, chose to experience life outside the classroom walls alone—refraining from accessing the auditory environment through an interpreter for fear of being socially stigmatized.

In discussing effective interpreters, all deaf students clearly identified the ally model of interpreting as being the most effective. The students collectively emphasized the need for the interpreter to clearly be their ally, aligned with the student rather than the hearing world. This finding seems reminiscent of the 1995 Allies Conference, in which deaf adults gave a similar message to the field of interpreting.

Finally, from the collective responses of the deaf students there emerged a strong theme of frustration in the lack of skill and professionalism of the substitute interpreters. When regular interpreters were not in school, most deaf students chose not to have an interpreter rather than risk having a substitute interpreter. Interestingly, the horror stories they told of substitute interpreters were based on the social harm caused to the student by the substitute's lack in understanding their social needs in the classroom.

Suggestions From Students

Several deaf students offered suggestions in improving how schools meet the needs of deaf students. These suggestions are currently being enacted in their own schools, and the deaf students find them to be very helpful. The suggestions focused on offering ASL as a foreign language, increasing collaboration between the deaf education teacher and the regular education classroom teacher, choosing teachers who are known to be flexible and welcoming to deaf students, and placing hearing students interested in learning sign language into the deaf student's classes. And yet it seemed clear that even with strong support structures, signing deaf students may still experience frustration. As one student reminded us, with the hearing and deaf students you have two different cultures, two very different sets of needs: "It's good for each group to learn about the other and interact with each other, but the basic needs are in conflict."

Unexpected Findings

Several unexpected topics emerged from the interviews. Several students shared concerns about the habits of cheating that their deaf education teacher and interpreters encouraged. Although the adults may have been perceived this "cheating" as simply making accommodations for the deaf student, this was clearly not the view of the students. In addition, several deaf students felt strongly that they were not receiving an appropriate education because their teachers, interpreters, and speech therapist were using valuable educational time to instead chat and engage in socializing with other adults. The deaf students were clearly angered by this disrespect for their education.

Another unexpected topic emerged from the responses of students who had experienced both mainstream and residential school learning environments. The strong preference for direct instruction, freedom in communication, and access to social experiences were expressed by students who had experienced both environments.

8 Interviews With Educational Interpreters

THE FOCAL POINT OF THIS STUDY was the voices of deaf children. But in addition, the perspectives of others in the educational setting are also helpful in gaining understanding of the intertwined dynamic of social interaction and communication. Since the interpreter is in the middle of most communicative acts, the interpreter's perspective seems particularly beneficial.

I interviewed ten interpreters for this study. The interpreters interviewed ranged from 26–58 years of age, and resided in Pennsylvania, Missouri, and Ohio. All interpreters have worked as educational interpreters in the K–12 setting (see Table 8.1). All interpreters have worked in large suburban school districts, and some interpreters have also worked in small rural school districts. All interpreters interviewed share a common experience of being bilingual in American Sign Language (ASL) and English. Eight of the interpreters have graduated from an interpreter training program, five are certified, and four also hold credentials as a teacher (see Table 8.2).

The interpreters' responses have been organized by topics. After presenting the responses for each topic, an interpretive section discusses the themes emerging within those responses. The final interpretive section presents a collective discussion of the major themes found throughout the interpreter interviews.

The names used are fictitious, and some additional identifying information has been changed to protect the identities of the participants. However, all the stories and vignettes are direct quotes from the interpreters.

Narrative Sketches of the Interpreters

Patricia: Patricia is a certified interpreter who has an extensive background in educational interpreting. Her experiences include 16 years of interpreting for deaf students from kindergarten through graduate school. She also has interpreted for a number of students with various special

Table 8.1 Professional Experiences of Interpreters

	Elementary	Middle school	High school
Patricia	X	X	X
Linda	X		
Kimberly	X	X	X
Kelly		X	
Toia	X	X	X
Mary		X	X
Cheryl			X
Cathy	X	X	X
Laurie	X	X	
Jean	X	X	X

Table 8.2 Education/Certifications of Interpreters

	Graduated from an interpreter-training program	Certified interpreter	Holds credentials as a deaf education teacher
Patricia	X	X	
Linda			X
Kimberly	X		
Kelly	X	X	

needs. Patricia has taught interpreting at the college level and has worked as a freelance interpreter for members of the adult deaf community. Patricia is a certified interpreter.

Linda: Linda has been involved in interpreting for nearly 16 years. She was initially a deaf education teacher and then later chose to change careers to become an educational interpreter. Her experiences have been mostly with elementary children and always in inclusion settings.

Kimberly: Kimberly learned sign language from a deaf childhood friend. She attended an interpreter training program and was hired as an educational interpreter after graduation. She has been interpreting for 5 years and has maintained a strong focus on promoting the social side of learning.

Kelly: While attending an interpreter training program, Kelly became actively involved in the deaf community. Since graduation, she has continued to be actively involved with deaf adults in her community. Kelly is a young interpreter and promotes professionalism among interpreters as a strong priority. She currently works both as a freelance interpreter and as an educational interpreter. Kelly is a certified interpreter.

Toia: Toia has both national and international experiences with deaf people. She has graduated from an interpreter training program and has since been hired as an educational interpreter. Her experiences include elementary school, middle school, and high school. She also has experience teaching at a school for the deaf.

Mary: Mary graduated from an interpreter training program. Since graduation, she has been actively involved in the deaf community through her church. She has now completed her second year as an educational interpreter in integrated schools.

Cheryl: Cheryl was first introduced to sign language through her husband's deaf parents. She later graduated from an interpreter training program and became certified. Cheryl maintains significant involvement in the deaf community through her church activities and serves in a leadership role in her school system.

Cathy: Cathy became interested in sign language as a teenager, when three deaf girls joined her Girl Scout troop. She followed her interest in college, where she gained the qualifications to be a deaf education teacher. However, she later decided to change career and become an educational interpreter. Soon after graduating from an interpreter training program, Cathy was hired as an educational interpreter.

Laurie: Laurie was a deaf education teacher and then graduated from the interpreting training program. She is a certified interpreter. She has contributed significantly to the DeafBlind community.

Jean: Jean has been working as an interpreter for over 25 years. She is certified and has a wealth of experience in both educational and freelance interpreting. She has maintained significant involvement in the deaf community through her local deaf church. She has also been active in organizing and managing camps for deaf children.

General Feelings About Deaf Students in Hearing Classrooms

Interpreters seem to have a front row seat in the daily lived experiences of deaf students in integrated educational environments. In this study, they were first asked to share their general feelings about placing deaf students in hearing schools. Their responses reveal interesting insight into their beliefs and opinions.

Kimberly

Overall, I think every student is different; every teacher is different. You have to take it one situation at a time. You can't have an attitude of, "This is my job, and this is best for everybody." In five years, I have been in three different schools and have had three very different experiences. So the biggest thing is to look at each situation individually. I've worked with kids that are very successful in regular ed. classes, doing social studies, chemistry, and all that stuff. I've also worked with a hard of hearing student in a life skills classroom [that represented] a totally different situation. I don't think I have ever worked with anyone who has had a horrible experience. I've had teachers that have made it more difficult.

Kelly

Do I see any redeeming factor in putting deaf kids in integrated classrooms? Not really. The teachers see them as "deaf kids," so it's almost as if they get pushed aside. Your reading is not up to par, "Well we'll just stick you in a reading group of your own," instead of really pushing them to improve. They seem to be getting left behind, like other kids with learning disabilities. Deafness is not a learning disability. It is a communication issue. I don't think most deaf kids are challenged. And then the deaf kids get a bad persona: "I'm no good, I'm just deaf. Why try?"

Patricia

I've had some very good experiences. We were very welcomed into the buildings that I have worked in. At first, I'm sure there was a lot of apprehension, but with the proper in-servicing, and making the teacher at ease, things went well.

Cathy

When you just have a few deaf kids in school, I see the only way they can succeed is that they have got to succeed with socializing with the hearing kids. With some that's OK, and with some that is a real big problem. But, the trend has continued of more and more parents keeping their hearing impaired children in their home district, which means they could often be the only deaf child in the building. They might even be the only hearing-impaired child in the whole district. If they can't make it socially with the hearing kids, they can be pretty isolated.

Laurie

We have an awesome program. I'm a teacher and I'm an interpreter. And I see both ends of what is going on. I just think this place is wonderful, and everybody should send their kids here. I love it—what can I say?

The interpreter responses ranged from positive to negative, with some centering on the understanding that every student is different. Some interpreters connected their enthusiasm for integrated education to their own positive feelings in the environment, while others tended to focus on the students' experiences. Patricia was inclusive in her comment, "We were very welcomed." Laurie also expressed personal satisfaction from her involvement in the program at her school when she said, "I just think this place is wonderful."

Kimberly had witnessed students succeeding and not succeeding, so she strongly urged others to not make generalized perspectives. Her measure for success of a deaf student rested on the student's ability to successfully engage in the higher academic coursework offered.

A deeper concern seemed to emerge from the responses of both Kelly and Cathy. Both seemed to recognize the themes of social isolation and inferiority that often follow deaf students into hearing classrooms. Overall, it seems that interpreters may have widely varying opinions on placing deaf students in integrated educational environments.

Accessing Education in the Regular Education Classroom

Toia

Most times, the hearing child goes into a history class, and they have so much background knowledge in history. They hear it all the time on television, or on the radio, or from family or friends talking about the Korean War or the Vietnam War. For the deaf child, they have no clue about what has happened because their grandparents don't sign, and their aunts and uncles don't sign. So they have no idea. I see deaf kids as at a great loss when they go into the classroom.

Education is imparted to students through a variety of means: direct instruction, cooperative learning, class discussion, recitation, student reports, etc. While hearing students can access these directly, deaf students may experience barriers in gaining access. The following quotes represent the interpreters' responses to the question the deaf students' ability to access the education offered in regular education classrooms.

Language

Kelly

I feel that the [deaf] kids do not understand me. Like one kid I worked with was a middle schooler and can't sign. Whenever he tries to communicate, he can only successfully communicate an idea by fingerspelling.

Jean

Hearing classroom meeting the needs of a Deaf student has its pros and cons. It all depends upon the Deaf student. Many students I have worked with have had minimal language skills, meaning their language is practically non-existent and their knowledge of sign language is a bare minimum, if that much. So most of their communication is done by mime with some sign language. A deaf student with MLS (minimal language skills) means that student's comprehension level isn't the same as a deaf student who is fluent in sign language. Therefore, the interpreter must come down to the level of the deaf student. Sometimes, that takes quite a bit of time for just one concept. Teachers not trained in deafness do not always understand all that's involved with working with this type of deaf student.

But, the skill level of my other students is totally awesome! I'm always learning new aspects of ASL from these students.

Mary

A lot of times you are with these kids all day, you don't know if they hear anything, and they know very little sign. Sometimes they are functioning like a second-grader when they are in ninth grade.

When I was an intern, when people found out I was in an interpreter training program, I got a lot of backlash because they were so anti-ASL in the schools. Even some of the deaf schools are not promoting ASL, but instead talk about total communication. And then they wonder why nobody has any language.

Accessing Content

Toia

I think the big negative for the deaf child is that the child's education is dependent on *my* level of education. It is what I know that I am able to impart to that child. The interpreting process is also dependent on my language skills—my knowledge of things of the world. Whatever subject I am interpreting for, my knowledge of that area is going to influence my interpretation for that student. Therefore, my abilities limit the child in what he or she learns.

Laurie

There is nothing that makes me feel any better than being in a classroom and seeing a deaf student laugh at the same time as their peers, or, to have them understand material and get the content.

Advocacy Skills

Kelly

Most students are unaware of their own rights and responsibilities. For example, if a student can't see, they need to let the teacher know. If a student doesn't understand what the teacher is saying, they need to inform the teacher. The student needs to let the interpreter know when he or she doesn't understand a specific sign or signing style.

Carol

Some students really do advocate for themselves: "I need this information." But some of them don't know that they can ask for that, or even should ask for that, so I do. The goal in school is to provide them the best educational experience you can.

Cheryl

Usually by the time they get to high school, these seniors will usually speak up for themselves. I try to empower them and so it is really good. Like last Thursday in chemistry class, the sub said to me, "Ask her if it is OK if I tell her two jokes." Well, the senior said, "Look at me, talk to me, I'll look at my interpreter and she'll tell me what you are saying, and then I'll look back at you." I'm thinking, "Yes! That is what is supposed to happen!"

The education in integrated classrooms might be quite good for hearing students, but the deaf student must be able to access it in order to learn. While some deaf students succeed in understanding the content of the class, others fail miserably. When discussing the concept of accessing education in the regular education classroom, interpreters spoke to three areas: language, content, and advocacy skills. From the responses of the interpreters, three issues emerged signaling significant barriers to access: minimal language skills of deaf students (both ASL and English), the interpreter's own knowledge and abilities, and the lack of self-advocacy skills.

The limited language skills of many deaf students, as recognized by Kelly, Jean, and Mary, would seem to have a perilous effect on their ability to learn through an interpreter. Jean seems to indicate that for these deaf students, the time necessary to explain a concept is not conducive to an integrated classroom, where the teacher moves on and does not understand the level of accommodation needed for this kind of student.

Why are so many deaf students lacking language skills, even in their own first language of ASL? Mary believes it may be linked to the strong anti-ASL stance she has witnessed in many schools. She seems to suggest that this stance has stripped deaf students of their right to language and has left them without any language through which to learn. Other factors leading to deaf students' low language skills may be in the language deprivation experienced by many students at home, where no one shares their language; or in schools where their peers and teachers can not communicate directly with them. Regardless, it does seem that the impact on the interpreting process is significant. Jean gives insight into the difficulty of interpreting for students with minimal language skills, requiring the interpreter to creatively incorporate both mime and sign to relate a concept. It also indicates that the role of the interpreter may extend from communication facilitator to language facilitator—someone who facilitates language development in the child. In all, the lack of language skills by many deaf students indicates a formidable barrier to their ability to access education in the integrated classrooms.

Another barrier identified was the limitations of the interpreters' skills, language, and knowledge. Toia believes that the use of an interpreter as a funnel for education will limit that education, depending upon the strengths and weaknesses of that interpreter. She feels limitations are imposed by the following four factors: the interpreter's knowledge of the language, knowledge of the world, knowledge of the subject, and level of education. She sees each of these factors as having profound influence on the educational outcomes of the student.

Finally, another obstacle students may experience in accessing education is their lack of advocacy skills. Kelly recognizes that some deaf students lack an understanding of their own rights and responsibilities, such as informing a teacher when they do not understand. Kelly's desire seems to be for deaf students to become more aggressive in accessing an education, rather than passively accepting a lower level of access.

Encouraging deaf students to advocate for their own rights is certainly a positive goal. When successful, it helps to give deaf students a sense of empowerment—such as in the example given by Cheryl. But the ability of deaf students to successfully advocate for themselves would seem to be highly dependent on a general feeling of already being empowered. Therefore, while teaching students to advocate for themselves is a goal to work towards, educators and parents must remain sensitive to the various obstacles that may prevent it, and they must continue to make accommodations for the needs of deaf students.

Overall, it seems clear that while some deaf students seem successful in accessing the education of the integrated classroom, others experience significant frustrations. According to the responses of interpreters in this study, barriers to access may emerge in the low language skills of deaf students, the limitations of interpreters, and the inability of deaf students to serve as effective advocates for their own education.

Through the following vignette, Mary brings to life the experiences of interpreters and deaf students in low-performing schools. Both the deaf student and the hearing students seem to be victims of poor educational decision-making. And both seem to have parallel home life conditions that make their education more of a struggle. Mary describes her own culture shock as she struggles to meet the needs of her deaf student in a hearing urban school.

"Deaf Kids in Bad Schools"

My current student is 18 years old. She is supposed to be in 11th grade, but they put her back into 10th grade for the past month, because she was behind. One of the biggest problems is that she wants out of school, but the mother wants her to stay in school so she can still get the SSI money. It's not like she is in school because her parents want her to get an education. She's on the 4th grade reading level. As you get older, you get discouraged and feel you don't know common things. But then again, this whole school seems to be way behind.

Sometimes schools neighboring each other can be very different. A lot of times, one school is wealthy, while another one next door doesn't have enough books.

In this school, most of them don't go to bed until 1 or 2 a.m. in the morning. You come to school and a lot of the students are lying on their desks sleeping.

The kids walk around in the hallways. The teachers don't want them, so they send them from homeroom to the library. Well, the other teacher says, "No, I don't want them either." So, the kid goes back and forth in the hallway for 20 minutes just killing time. There is not a lot of discipline. It is a culture shock for me.

I hear the teacher talking about how they have to keep watering down the subjects. These kids just can't grasp it. Like my deaf child, she reads on the 4th grade level, and she can probably read better than a lot of kids in her classroom. I asked today, are there any academics in this school? They said, "Oh yeah, we have some, like the biology class." But the teacher said they don't dissect anything. She said, "I would be afraid to give them knives. I'm afraid they would all be around me with little scalpels pointed at me!" She said they had to water the biology class down.

Continued

If they don't learn English the first time through, then they send them back down to the younger grades. The teacher said, "I had a good group of kids learning, but now I have these bigger bad kids put in my room, and they cause a lot of stuff and are very disruptive." It is just like chaos. The kids sit up on the windowsills.

I've seen deaf kids crying and saying, "I'm afraid, my mom and dad are coming. I am afraid of them. I come to school because I am afraid." I think, "Oh no, I'm not prepared for this." To a lot of people in these schools, this is just so common. And then I hear "Oh, my mom never showed up at home. I've been staying home alone for 2 or 3 days." So, they can't do their projects for class. When you are not used to that, it is just like a different culture.

So these children, none of them can afford hearing aids. So, they may have an FM system at school, but then they take it off and have nothing at home.

—Mary

Accessing the Full School Environment

What kinds of information is not interpreted for deaf students? And what impact do these omissions have on the experiences of deaf students?

In what ways do deaf students receive or not receive full access to their school environments?

Kimberly

There is no way that you can provide full access to everything. At the beginning of class and the kids are all coming in, and they are all talking about different things. I might be able to pick up one or two little things and I'll say, "This is funny, you may want to know . . . " and I'll tell them. But there is no way I can tell them everything that is happening in the room. If you miss something, you can't always say, "Can you say that again?" You lose a lot of the context in doing that.

I think the important stuff is generally interpreted. But there is a lot of little incidental stuff that isn't interpreted. They say . . . 90% of what you learn is incidental learning. There is a lot of it that just doesn't get interpreted. I don't know that you can really put blame on it, it's just because we are human.

Patricia

Certainly in the bathroom, those conversations do not get interpreted. And that is where a lot of probably great conversations take place with regular education kids. Ha! Lunchroom conversation does not get interpreted, either. And as I mentioned earlier, having friends that can sign is crucial for the social well-being of the deaf student. It is necessary for the interpreter to go to the lunchroom on occasion, for example, on the first day of school, when all the lunchroom rules will be explained. Also, to introduce yourself to the cafeteria workers and lunchroom aides. Let them know where to find you in the event they need to make a special announcement or just need to speak to the deaf student. And in the hall, a lot of times deaf students don't want to walk with us.

Kelly

The deaf child doesn't get access, period. Because they don't hear kids laughing. They don't hear kids making bodily function noises. And a lot of interpreters don't give them that. Just like every day normal sounds. There is none of that interpreted. I've worked with students when I've said . . . "I can hardly hear because the fan is really loud." The student replies "What fan?" Or, the teacher has this funky accent and sometimes they say a word different. Everyone else in the class laughs, but the deaf kids don't have a clue. They'll say, "Well I never knew that."

So, there again, you are isolating the kid. They are not getting what everyone else is getting. And no matter what you do, you can never give that, either.

Toia

Side conversations are not interpreted in the classroom. Sometimes we are in the classroom sitting, and the teacher is lecturing, and students are having side conversations, while the teacher is still talking. Most times, that gets eliminated. It is hard for the interpreter to keep track of what the side conversations are, as well as the teacher's lecture.

A child having an interpreter in the classroom is not necessarily giving them full access, because [the interpreter] is only an individual in the classroom, and if 10 different people are talking at the same time, then we are incapable of providing access in that situation. What we have to do is stick to one conversation or the main conversation, and provide access to that. But these nine other conversations get eliminated.

The interpreters seem to collectively insist that full access is impossible. They qualify their lack of ability to provide full access by explaining their human incapacity to hear and represent a multitude of voices and sounds at one time. They give examples of numerous language interactions and auditory environmental stimulus both inside and outside the classroom walls that are not interpreted and therefore not accessible to deaf students. These uninterpreted language acts include conversations in the bathroom, hall, and lunchroom—the places where relationship building among peers seems to be most active. Therefore, it would seem that deaf students lack access in the places where hearing students are most actively involved in the complex social systems of student culture. Thus, the lack of access could likely lead to the social deprivation of deaf students in integrated settings.

The lack of access to other auditory stimulus can also be limiting. Hearing people make assumptions and judgments based on the way people talk—the tone of voice they use, their accent, and the words they choose. Since deaf students do not have access to those elements, the power is given to the interpreter to make the judgments and decide whether to withhold or share that information with the deaf student.

When multiple voices are occurring, it might be tempting to place a single priority on giving the deaf student access to the teacher's voice. However, from a social constructivist perspective all voices hold value. In an educational environment, the complexity among voices brings deeper insight and learning. Therefore the social constructivist perspective would seem to support the value of all voices of collaboration, interaction, and relationship building—many of which deaf children do not have access to.

Overall, it seems clear that the deaf student is not able to access the full school environment. Without access to the authentic range of language acts and auditory environmental stimuli represented in the school, the deaf student is given a very different experience. Some of the areas that are inaccessible to deaf students seem to be the most active areas of relationship building and connecting with student culture for hearing students. Therefore, it seems clear that through lack of access, deaf students are subjected to social and language deprivation in integrated educational settings.

Another indicator of social deprivation emerges in the vignette, "Who's Talking About Me?" Living in a world they cannot fully access, and they do not fully understand, deaf students may have the psychotic notion that others are talking about them. Again, it is another indicator of the abnormal milieu created when deaf students are in socially and linguistically deprived settings.

"Who's Talking About Me?"

Some deaf kids think that any time the hearing kids are talking, they think they are talking about them. It's not just the other kids. They might think that the teachers are talking about them. Especially if someone just happens to glance over at them. They can be just a little bit paranoid.

—Linda

Interaction and Relationship Building Between Deaf and Hearing Students

The interpreters were all asked to share their insights into the communication and relationship building between deaf students and hearing students. Since interpreters are often in the middle of such relationships, their magnified vantage point provides clear insight and greater understanding into the complexities of these relationships. The interpreters' responses are organized into the following categories: communication/conversation topics, hearing students learning sign language, relationship building, dating, deaf students choosing friends, and acceptance.

Communication / Conversation Topics

Patricia

I think that the kids tend to talk about things that we might consider risqué, especially when they get to a middle school level. And, the hearing kids are comfortable talking about that with each other. But if you have an interpreter in the mix, certainly the conversation is not going to be about anything risqué, like matters of the opposite sex. . . .

[Once] a deaf student became involved in a risqué conversation in the lunchroom and decided to write their comments to ensure that they were being understood. When the volume went up, the adults became suspicious, the paper was confiscated, and the deaf student was punished for what they had written. Lesson learned . . . careful about what you write, but not necessarily about what you say!

So I think that it is really best when the kids are learning their language and able to pick up those things. This way they can converse directly with the deaf child, who might have a desire to talk about those things at that level, with all the hormones raging and whatnot. I think it is important that they are able to share that with someone at their own level.

Kelly

You don't see much interaction outside class work. With the hearing kids, they have the chatter on the side with friends, but the deaf student is just not there. The deaf student is kind of like the loner of the group.

The hearing kids will talk with them in class. . . . "OK, we have an assignment to do, let's work in groups, come work with us." But that is where it ends. Even during group time it's really hard, because then the hearing students get the whispers going. But that student is kind of left out. And I can't say, "Excuse me, can you speak up, so I can interpret what you are saying?" because that's not what they're trying to do. They are trying to have their own conversation.

So it separates, it is not an intimate relationship, like hearing kids with hearing kids have. It's not "Let's talk about the boys" or "I can't believe what that teacher is doing" or whatever. It's so distant and shallow.

Do the kids understand the interpreting process? Some kids will say "Oh, OK, it's just between us, so the interpreter is not there." But then, they'll say, "Will you tell her . . . " I say, "She is standing right there. You tell her, and I will be interpreting so she understands you." "Well . . . will you tell her . . . " They just do not understand that the communication is between the two of them.

Linda

Hearing kids do not really talk to the deaf kids about the same topics as they do with each other. If the deaf student is really profound, it is probably more like, "thumbs up" or "Good Job" and point to their paper, or they will show them a picture and they'll laugh. They don't really have in-depth conversations.

We have one profoundly deaf child now. He actually interacts fairly well with everyone at recess. He has two pretty good friends. But a lot of their communication is like . . . "Hey . . . how are you . . . hello . . . good-bye." They play games, but I'm not sure how much they actually understand each other

Toia

The hearing kids use the interpreter to only communicate on a very basic level with the deaf kids. They may ask, "How are you? Did you have a good day? How's the homework?" But they generally only talk about school things. They don't get into any details, or talk about girls and boys, and that kind of thing. They don't share any intimate things with the deaf students.

Jean

The language barrier is really on the hearing student's part. The deaf student doesn't seem to have a problem of trying to communicate. The hearing student isn't accustomed to this type of communication and often will withdraw

Kimberly

There are certain hearing kids that only talk to the deaf students about school. But some of it is their personality. There is one girl who is good in signing, but she never talks to the deaf student about anything but school, school, school. But I look at some of these other girls who have only very basic limited signs, and they try to talk to her about so many other things: boys, dances, sports, "Oh my gosh, guess what happened this morning." I mean this hearing student [the one that joins us for lunch] will say "Oh my gosh, Josh kissed me at the dance!" And my deaf student will say, "Oh my gosh!"

Laurie
> The students that are hard of hearing, they interact well. They don't seem to have a lot of trouble. But some of the students that are on the deaf end of the spectrum may have a little more trouble, but they make an effort.
>
> The hard of hearing students seems to be more comfortable making that leap, and the deaf students are not as comfortable making that leap. But on the other hand, there are some deaf students who go up and interact all of the time. It depends on the student. It is not a language or social thing. It is "Are you shy?" It is not always a language issue.

Two themes emerge through the comments of the interpreters concerning communication between hearing and deaf students. First, the communication between deaf and hearing students is quite limited in scope and depth. While hearing students speak to each other about a range of topics, they tend to discuss only school with the deaf students. The interpreters described the conversations between hearing and deaf peers as distant, shallow, and lacking intimacy. For example, Linda explains that the signing deaf students may only communicate with peers through a thumbs up and pointing system. Interestingly, the only exception was found in Kimberly's comments; she sees her deaf student as having much deeper involvement in the social system and related conversations of the school. But it is important to note that Kimberly invites the deaf and hearing students to eat lunch in the resource room every day so that she can facilitate language learning and communication on a daily basis. Therefore, the communication between this deaf student and her hearing peers may be much deeper and more varied than it is for other deaf students.

A second theme is found in the hearing students' lack of understanding of the interpreting process. This theme was also noted by the deaf students. When students do not understand the interpreting process, they feel they are having a conversation with an interpreter, not through an interpreter. This phenomenon creates even further emotional distance between the deaf and hearing students. Overall, the limited language exchange between deaf and hearing students is a clear indicator of the language deprivation and social isolation experienced by the hearing students.

Hearing Students Learning Sign Language

Mary
> One girl said, "Oh, I know sign." She talked to her [the deaf student] once, and said "Hi." That was the end of it. Sometimes they say, "Hey, I know the

alphabet!" and then they show them the alphabet. That is about the end of the communication.

Jean

Generally the hearing students will write down their conversation to the deaf student. This is true for the majority of the time; not often am I included in the conversation. Generally, the hearing students become very intrigued by sign language and will begin asking questions how to sign different words. Eventually, the deaf student begins to teach/show sign language to the hearing student. Then they will either write down the conversation or a mixture of signs and writing down the conversation especially if one or the other isn't understanding what was signed.

Patricia

I think that you are lucky if you have, across the grade level, two students who are able to learn to sign well enough to converse fluently at that level. They are fortunate if they can be in the classroom with the deaf child. They are able to sit and watch you, if the teacher permits it, while you are interpreting. You almost establish a mentor-like relationship with those hearing children where they are constantly asking you for feedback, "Why did you sign it that way? Or why didn't you sign it this way?" It really keeps us on our toes as interpreters whenever the kids become fluent.

Cathy

A couple of kids who are in classes where I am working now, they haven't really learned a lot of sign, but they have found that they can point, with a lot of gesturing and body language, and they are actually having some social contact.

Kelly

Hearing students don't learn much sign language. If they do, it's usually fingerspelling. Well, on the 2nd grade level, when kids are trying to fingerspell, you can't really communicate that way. I have seen kids try, but that is still not an intimate conversation. You can't just know two or three signs and have a conversation: "OK let's talk about boys . . . well, I don't know signs for that." "Let's talk about the football game . . . PLAY FOOTBALL." That's it! There is no in-depth conversations. Like in middle school, hearing students are always on the phone and talking, "Oh my goodness, can you believe what he said about her." Well, for deaf kids, you have that communication barrier.

Cheryl

Sometimes kids think of it as a novelty, and a few kids might want to learn sign language. But I think as time goes on, they lose their patience with that deaf student, especially if that deaf student keeps asking them, "What did they say? What did they say?" One of the kids will become their interpreter or their voice. I think that would be hard for a deaf kid, being the only one . . . isolated.

Toia

There is not much of a relationship between deaf and hearing students. I find it is hard for the hearing students to really communicate directly on any level with the deaf student, because the hearing students do not have enough language skills to communicate fluently with them. Many times, the effort of trying to communicate is frustrating to both the hearing child and the deaf child. Learning a second language is a barrier to communication, because they do not take the time to learn their language.

Linda

Some hearing kids do learn how to sign really well. But I don't really see it much in the elementary school, because they are so little. But I've known some kids that do. Sometimes, these kids tell me what the deaf kids say. Sometimes, I guess, but not always.

The interpreters' responses indicate that few hearing students learn sign language well enough to have a conversation with deaf students and that most communication between deaf and hearing students involves gesturing and pointing. While some students will learn to sign the alphabet or a few signs, this is not sufficient for them to have a conversation. Fingerspelling can create an even greater barrier, because hearing students feel that they have made the leap to communicating in the deaf student's language. They are perplexed when the deaf student doesn't understand. However, deaf students struggle with the English language, most often because they have never *heard* it. Since they do not have the full capacity to use phonics to sound out words, learning to spell is often based on sheer memorization. Therefore, fingerspelling is not necessarily more helpful to deaf students, especially young deaf students.

The second theme that is evident in the interpreter's responses is the enormous amount of time and patience that is required of the deaf student, in order to teach a hearing student sign language. This theme also emerged in the interview of Julie, a deaf student, when she said,

It is so hard to teach other people to communicate. I mean, I'm happy to help people learn how to communicate with me but it takes so long until they get fluent. It takes a lot of effort, and I'm a bit tired of working so hard just to have friends I can talk with.

Though it is a long, arduous process for the deaf student, the hearing students that are willing to learn sign language, and are fortunate enough to find a deaf student that will teach them, are the beneficiaries of a full language—the gift of bilingualism. Kimberly's story offers some hope that this is possible.

"Teaching a Foreign Language at Lunch"

I can remember one hearing girl coming up to me in the hallway and saying, "I want to learn sign so bad, can you teach me sign".

I told her, "Well now, I don't have time to sit down and teach you an entire foreign language, but why don't you come have lunch with us?"

That is how it started. I thought this girl would come maybe once a week, but every day she is in there eating lunch with us. Every day! Now, that may not work with some kids, but some just need that little push to help them find out they have something in common with these [deaf] kids.

The friendship between this girl and the deaf student started on the [school sports] team. Now, they have a lot in common and their communication is improving.

Relationship Building

Kelly

I still think there is a level of relationship that they are not getting. And many of them go home and get *nothing* until they come back to school the next day. For example, no one is saying at lunch, "Hey why don't you come to my house after school?" "Hey come sleep over at my house this weekend." There is just not that level of communication. The hearing kids and deaf kids just don't communicate that well, and the interpreter can't go on the sleepover with them.

I think every kid is different. But if I had to say a percentage, I think the majority of them are very lonely, even if they act macho, and give people the idea, "You can't hurt me."

Kimberly

The deaf student I work with now has made several new friends this year—upperclassmen—that think she is just the coolest thing. They come in and eat lunch with us; they want to hang out with her. I'm sure there are other hearing kids that don't even acknowledge her. She is in the room, but they don't go running up to talk to her. I think it is 50/50—either the kids really like her, and they make more of an effort, or they want nothing to do with her. I don't think there is a whole lot of in between. They are either your friend or they are not. The other hearing kids might have acquaintances, where I don't think the deaf kids do. They either have their friends, or they don't.

But at the high school level I wonder . . . they are good friends in school, but do they chat outside of school? Do they talk on the phone? Do they go to the mall? Do the hearing kids make that attempt to include them outside of school?

Cathy

I think for the most part, the hearing kids are a little apprehensive about the deaf kids. The kids who come to high school, and have never seen an interpreter or met a deaf person, they are a little afraid because it is different. Unless they are a pretty outgoing or accepting person, they tend to ignore the deaf person. I don't see a lot of actively putting them down or anything, they just kind of ignore them.

Toia

I don't know of the hearing kids and the deaf kids doing anything together outside of school. Yes, the deaf kids are involved in school activities, but all communication is only about the school activities. They are not going out together.

What kinds of relationships occur between deaf students and hearing students? Though some good friendships may emerge, it seems from the responses of the interpreters that the majority of their relationship building falls into two categories: deaf students seen as novelties and deaf students ignored. The deaf student, Jasmine, also observed this superficial interest of hearing students when she said, "Well, it seemed I had a lot of friends in hearing school who were my age. But they're not my friends, if they try to take advantage of deaf people. They just want to learn sign language to look cool."

In regarding deaf students and sign language as novelties, hearing students' interest may remain high for a time. But they most likely will still not include deaf students in their time outside of school. Also, their interest may be often relatively short lived.

Several interpreters also explained that many hearing students simply ignore deaf students. They may be polite toward them, but they do not choose to interact with them. By treating deaf students as though they are invisible, hearing students do not have to confront the awkwardness of the communication barrier.

"Politeness, not Friendship"

Sometimes it seems it's a mutual agreement between the deaf and hearing students. The deaf kids are just *there*. It's like they are thinking, "OK, we'll say 'Hi' and you smile; if I have to talk to you, I will." I think the deaf students are very isolated.

Continued

The hearing kids might come to me and ask a simple question, "Ask her what she is making." When I ask the deaf student, they say, "You *know* what I am making." I'll say, "Yes, I know, but they asked." The deaf student will say, "I already told you, so just tell them." They kind of wipe it off, too.

Some kids are a little more friendly. But even then, it's like they are saying to the deaf student, "I know you are different, and I'll be polite to you."

It is politeness, and not friendship.

—Mary

Dating

Kimberly

I don't see a whole lot of deaf/hearing boy/girl relationships occurring in the mainstream situation. I think the obvious reason is the communication issue. Who wants to date someone they can't communicate directly with? I don't think the kids like the idea of dating a person that they'd have to go through a third party to talk with. I've seen friendly flirting go on, but it doesn't go much further than that. I think it's probably viewed [by the hearing student] as more trouble than it's worth.

Dating seems to be the gateway into the social realm of many high schools. Therefore, the lack of a dating relationship may be indicative of more than not having a dating relationship. It may also mean that the deaf student is not aware and not part of the social networks in the school. In the deaf student section, Jasmine confirms the feelings of being left out in dating when she states, "It's different at the hearing school; it is hard to have friends and boyfriends because they aren't like me to start with." The exclusion of deaf students in the dating realm is reflective of their overall social isolation.

"High School Dating Scene"

I have a student who [communicates through] ASL, but she has quite a few friends. She is athletic, she is very self-confident, she is academically quite bright and hard working. She has very few long-term close friends, but she has many acquaintances that she is very friendly with. And they'll "high five" her in the hall, and they say, "I need to copy these notes, I missed class," which is very normal interaction in high school.

Continued

> But I would be surprised if a hearing boy would suddenly ask her to a dance or something, because that is more than everybody can manage. If there is no one else in the building using ASL, the deaf student is left out [of the dating scene]. They are really pretty isolated. It would be pretty unusual to go out with someone that you really couldn't communicate with.
>
> —Cathy

How do deaf students choose friends?

Kimberly

I think deaf students choose friends basically by who learns sign language. There might be the kids that have been in school together since kindergarten, so we wave at each other in the hallway. We can encourage the kids to learn how to sign, but I think it really does mean the deaf kids are limited by who does learn sign. In schools with more than one deaf student, the deaf students all tend to stick together, because they can communicate with each other.

It often depends on how sign dependent they are. A lot of them who are mainstreamed are [speaking deaf students]. They can often communicate directly with the hearing students a little bit better. So they have a wider choice in who they make friends with. But the kids who are sign dependent that don't communicate much orally, they tend to be friends with someone who is willing to learn sign.

The consensus among most interpreters is that deaf students choose friends based on who learns sign language. The speaking deaf students have more choices for friendships because the signing deaf students are limited by who learns their language. How many hearing students learn sign language? The signing deaf students and interpreters reported that even in the best cases, only two hearing students learned sign language well enough to have a direct conversation with the deaf student. Therefore, the deaf student is limited to these two students to develop friendships.

How do hearing students choose friends? They usually base friendships on shared interests. For example, horse lovers will find other horse lovers, and so on. However, among students there is often an on-again, off-again quality in their relationships, especially among girls. While upset with one friend, they may find solace in another, but later return to the first.

For deaf students, it seems obvious that the natural rhythm of finding and developing friendships is severely limited. Not only are they limited to who learns sign language, but also they are limited in their ability to break the friendship when it becomes uncomfortable. This point also emerged in Julie's interview: "But now [my best friend and I] have arguments and disagreements. She's the one who starts the fights, I put up with her because she's the only one I can communicate with and it is so hard to teach other people to communicate."

This limitation seems to be a direct indicator of the social isolation that deaf students experience. It also seems to reveal the level of lack of power that deaf student hold—even in their own friendships.

Acceptance

Kimberly

The kids that [have normal cognitive abilities] seem to be accepted a little bit better than the multiple disabilities. This one girl had a hearing loss, plus other problems. That is a whole other issue in being accepted.

Linda

A lot of the kids I interpret for now are more hard of hearing—almost more hearing than not. Those kids very easily blend in with the hearing kids.

Toia

The social needs of the hearing students and the social needs of the deaf student . . . there is a big difference because the deaf student does not always feel as though their social needs are being met. Again, language is the barrier. The internal H: struggles that deaf students have, the hearing students are not aware of it. For them, it is always "I'm not good enough, I have to try to fit into your world, but you are not trying to fit into my experiences," and I see that the deaf students are always struggling when it comes to their social interaction.

Kelly

Do the parents take pride in their child? Or, do they have an attitude of "We have to *fix* you. We don't want you to be deaf. You aren't really deaf!"

It tells the kid they are not good enough for them. But worse, this idea is reinforced again and again at school. It's reinforced when no one can communicate with them in school. It is reinforced in their grades, because of a reading issue. Or when there is not a skilled interpreter to help them in that communication barrier. You have *all of that* telling the kid, "You're not important, because you are deaf."

Cathy

The higher the deaf kids goes academically, the more likely they are to be accepted socially. When you are in a higher track, [hearing] kids have more self-confidence, and are often emotionally more stable. So, they are more able to adjust to someone who is different and more willing to take the time to do so.

The hearing kids are really involved in this huge social competition. And, the deaf kids aren't as aware of it, and don't participate in it as much. The hearing kids are talking about who went to whose house on Friday night, what movies they are going to, what music they just bought. . . . It does seem that the boys do fit in a bit easier. Even in high school, the boys do a lot of roughhousing, but the social world of hearing girls is so based on talking to each other, and these finely developed social networks, that it would be an extraordinary deaf girl that could fit into that, I think.

A real plus too, is if you are involved in sports. It gives you a common interest, and the kids who are athletic tend to have a better time getting accepted, too.

Mary

I've been in classrooms where the deaf kids were in honors math, physics, and everything, but they are still not accepted. This one child could talk well, and didn't need an interpreter much, but because her voice is a little funny, she is not accepted.

I see [these deaf kids] as a whole different culture. I don't see them as part of deaf culture or hearing culture. I think they are so isolated.

Jean

Once they realize the deaf student really isn't any different than they are and it's just another way of communicating, they really seem to be accepting of the deaf student. Hearing students may be shy or intimidated by sign language because they don't know what is being said. However, they do think it's quite "cool" once they understand it is a way of communication or it's another language. There have been numerous of times the hearing students think it's so awesome how I'm able to tell the deaf student everything they are saying.

Interpreters spend their days working closely with deaf students, and they witness the experiences and characteristics that shape deaf students' lives. During each interview, interpreters were asked to describe their observations. The responses reveal a continuum of acceptance for deaf students (see Figure 8.1).

Multihandicapped	Signing deaf students	Speaking deaf Students
Less accepted		More accepted

Figure 8.1   Hearing Students' Acceptance of Deaf Students

Cathy felt that deaf students in academically advanced classes were more likely to be accepted, but Mary disagreed. She emphasized that even higher-achieving speaking deaf students are often not accepted, but rather are excluded because of their differences.

The interpreters identified deaf students with both good and poor self-esteem. The students with healthy, positive self-esteem were described as being bold and somewhat macho, while "giving people the idea, 'You can't hurt me.'" Some interpreters thought that these students were successful, while others worried that it was a coping mechanism and these kids were still struggling with feelings of loneliness.

The interpreters were particularly concerned for the students with low self-esteem. Kelly's response sheds light on the possible reasons that these deaf students feel inferior. Her comments reinforce the theme of oppression, as everyone in the student's life makes that child feel inferior. Her insight mirrors the experiences shared in the interviews of many of the deaf students.

In all, though a few deaf students have positive self-esteem, most suffer from feelings of inferiority and social isolation. These negative feelings may originate in the inferiority and oppression embedded into the lives of deaf students from multiple sources. The vignette, told by Kelly, brings this concept to life.

"The McDonald's Syndrome"

A problem I see in the mainstream, involves a child's speech. I have witnessed several instances where a student is told by those on the deaf ed. team [deaf ed. teacher, speech therapist, etc.] that their speech is clear and easily understood.

However, when that student enters the mainstream, or public setting, people have a hard time understanding them, which leads to frustration and misunderstanding for both the deaf and hearing individuals.

An example from my own experiences: A deaf student asked the interpreter (who was familiar with the speech of that student) about picking *straws* for an activity. The interpreter had to ask three times for clarification because she heard the words "bra" and "sex." Finally, on the fourth try, after prompting the student to speak slowly, the interpreter was finally able to understand the student. I think this is an injustice for the students because they believe the whole world can understand them when that is not the case.

—Kelly

Promoting Social Experiences for Deaf Students

How do interpreters promote interaction, relationship building, and a connectedness with others for deaf students in hearing schools? Their varied responses are presented in the quotes below.

Kelly

I don't think they can promote friendship. I don't think there is any way to do that. The communication just is not there on that level. And no middle schooler or high schooler is going to tell an interpreter, "I want to tell [the deaf student] a secret. Tell them to come here." That is just not very common, in my experience. In my experience, it has only happened when the students are in a contest, and you don't want the opposing team to hear. That is the *only* situation that I have ever been in that the deaf person was involved at any intimate level. But as a teacher, I don't think you can bridge that gap. You can show, yourself, that you accept that student, but that doesn't allow you to connect other people intimately.

Kimberly

The interpreter has a lot to do with supporting the social needs of the deaf students. I try to chat with the kids, to pull [the deaf student] in. Say one of the kids is coming up and talking to us. If we are right there, I will interpret the conversation so that they know, and I'll say, "You know that happened to me." Just to try to make that connection. Because I think that has so much to do with them getting involved in conversations. If you have an interpreter who just sits there and doesn't do anything but interpret what is being said, you are missing an opportunity.

I think deaf kids in public schools, they need the encouragement to make friends. The deaf education teacher and I will sit and teach the kids some sign. And that is why I think it goes back to the interpreter and the teacher of the deaf needing to encourage that relationship.

The hearing girls that eat lunch with us are always talking about who likes who, and who's dating who. It so hard to keep it straight, and the Deaf student doesn't always know everyone they are referring to by name. [The deaf ed. teacher and I] decided to create a chart using photocopied pictures from the yearbook to create what we call the "Dating Chart." We copied, laminated, and attached velcro to each picture so that they can be moved (you know how teenagers are) around on the piece of poster board. It's a fun visual way for the Deaf student to keep up with who's who and what's going on.

Cathy

I am there with the same group of kids every day, and some time I do help initiate [relationships between hearing and deaf student]. Get something started that is not happening that could be or should be happening. I had one student who was just extraordinarily shy. If I hadn't started by making the contact with the hearing kid, nothing would have ever happened. I have plenty of kids who are more outgoing. They initiate it, and if things aren't going well, I may interpret and help out. But often I don't need to.

Interpreters often build the communication bridge between hearing students and deaf students. But is it possible to foster friendships? Kimberly believes it is. She sees the fostering of friendships as one of her primary responsibilities. Cathy shares that she also fosters relationships between deaf and hearing students. But Kelly counters that you can't promote intimacy. She feels that the communication barrier is too great. In all, it seems that interpreters and teachers can be active in promoting social interaction between deaf and hearing students, although they may not be able to encourage true intimacy. But by creatively finding ways to connect deaf students and hearing students socially, they can foster friendships. By teaching sign language to hearing students, they can enlarge the deaf students' social circle. However, the level of intimacy must ultimately depend on the level of language learning by the hearing student.

But Kimberly has found success in promoting friendships. By inviting hearing students to join the deaf student and her for lunch, she has been able to create a social circle for the deaf student. Success seems to be evident throughout her interview.

Some deaf students believe that they experience greater social interaction when their interpreter can fit in as a student. Kimberly fits this mold and is aware of it:

> I also think [as an interpreter] being young has a lot to do with it, too. I think a lot of these kids see me on their level. The girls come in at lunchtime, and they are telling me stuff that sometimes I'm like . . . Oh gosh, I'm not a student, they treat me like another student. But I think that makes it easier for them to accept the deaf student.

Interaction and Relationship Building Between the Deaf Student and the Interpreter

Interpreters often speak of their struggle between developing a professional relationship with their client (the student) and their heart tug to be a friend to a lonely child who needs someone to talk to who shares their language. Toia expressed this very well:

It is very hard for an interpreter. While the teacher expects the interpreter to be a professional, the deaf student expects the interpreter to be their peer or friend. You have to be treading on a very fine line. You have to maintain your professionalism, but at the same time, you don't want to have a student who is a misfit in the school and not having anyone to interact with.

Although the distinction in this section is between the terms *professional* and *friendship* orientation, it should be clearly noted that friendship-oriented interpreters can be highly effective and highly professional. The distinction might best be thought of in the allies model. The professional interpreters are more aligned with the hearing adults, and the friendship-oriented interpreters are more aligned with the deaf students.

Comments From a Professional Orientation

Patricia

I think is very important that the kids call us Mr. or Mrs. I think we need to establish some amount of professional distance, because not only are we in the role of being an interpreter, but we are also teaching the role of the interpreter. I really prefer not to be considered a friend to the kids. It is really hard not to cross that line at times, though. But I think the kids have more of a tendency for disrespect when you allow your guard to drop and end up being their friend. I think there still needs to be a professional distance.

Linda

They don't see me as a friend. I don't think it helps to be their friend. I can see why you might have more of a tendency to have that if they were older, but these kids are younger. I don't think they need a friend. They need someone there to tell them what they are supposed to be doing. I play games with them, I joke with them, but I'm not their friend. If I try to be their friend, then pretty soon I'm going to have to say, "OK you've got to stop and pay attention." You can't be both . . . their buddy and then . . . the boss. I think in the back of their minds they need to know that I am the boss. I'll laugh with you, and we'll have fun, but when it comes down to it, I am the boss. And when I tell you to do something, you had better do it. I am the boss . . . and you are not the boss of me.

Kelly

It is really hard, because they are only kids, and they look lost. And they just want someone to talk to. But yet, if you allow that to happen, that just isolates them more. Like it doesn't push them to reach out to others.

But, "No, your job is to act as a professional interpreter. Your job is to dress appropriately. Your job is to act appropriately, not to mingle with the kids. You are not there to be their friends. You are there to be their interpreter." I see that a lot, and it is sad, because other people outside of the profession (teachers, principals) see that too. They don't see any reason to see us as professionals.

Cathy

They like to chat with you because you are the person they can chat with. But I try to remember that I am the adult and I am the professional and I am not their friend, though I am very friendly with them. I not going to be their best friend, I don't want to be their best friend. I have 50-year-old best friends, because that is what I am. I think I have good rapport with my students, but I don't meet them at the mall to go shopping. They are not my friend. We get along well at school, and we work well together at school to accomplish what we need to do, so that they will be successful in school, but certainly we are friendly. When you spend that much time with somebody, you are going to have a lot of small talk. But I think I have a clear boundary that this is a professional relationship.

I can think of some individuals who do way too much involvement in the student's social life. But that is only a few. Most of them are pretty focused on academics. I've seen people trying to arrange dates, and that's really inappropriate in my opinion. I've seen interpreters going clothes shopping, meeting them for lunch, or having them to their apartment for dinner. It's not just the teacher, some of the interpreters do that too. They get too emotionally involved, and they do become their friend or try to arrange their life.

Laurie

I feel like the student knows I am an adult and a professional in the building, but at the same time we can interact and have fun—not while class is going on. Today a student finished their work, and I did have a conversation, but the hearing students were having little conversations, so it wasn't an inappropriate moment for me to have a conversation. But we can joke around and have a good time, so I think there is a mix and there is a blend. You and the student have to know when it is a time you need to be professional, and when it is a time you can joke around. Some don't understand that distinction, and some do.

I do not socialize with the students outside of school. I don't give them my phone number, I don't carry on conversations outside of school time, unless, you know, it is an after-school activity for which I am interpreting. But, I don't want to be so rigid, that I come across as being unapproachable, either.

Cheryl

I don't see [the pull between being a professional and being a student's friend]. We have so many sports programs, after school activities, and the deaf kids have a lot more exposure to social experiences. Also, they interact with kids from the school for the deaf and other kids on Wednesday each week at a local deaf church. They have lots of things to do, and other friends to be with outside of school. In our town, a local organization has Deaf Teens Club, and Deaf Kids Club. That is once a month at the YMCA. They have a speaker, activities, and refreshments. Different organizations support it. And, several of the deaf kids that are isolated in the deaf programs out of town can come together for that time. The kids in our area are very fortunate because they have lots of opportunities outside of school.

Clearly, many interpreters have very strong feelings about maintaining a level of professionalism as an interpreter. From their perspective, they lose the respect of both students and adults in the building when they engage in friendships within the school. Although these interpreters have a strong orientation to professionalism, it is also important to note that many of them also engage in playful joking around and side conversations when appropriate. Several interpreters who are strongly oriented toward professionalism are perplexed by their colleagues who engage in friendships with deaf students and spend time with deaf students outside of school. Overall, these interpreters felt it was best for the field to maintain a professional relationship with both students and other adults in the building.

Another interesting dimension was revealed in Cheryl's response. When deaf students have multiple opportunities to build relationships with other deaf students, they no longer long for a friendship relationship with their interpreters. Cheryl's community has creatively found ways to engage deaf students in positive social structures outside of the school environment.

Comments From a Friendship Orientation

Patricia

On the other hand, the younger students want to hold your hand going down the hall, and kind of show you off a bit. Especially those children who don't have anyone at home who signs, they develop a deep relationship with their interpreters.

Kimberly

I think [from a deaf student's perspective], you have this person with you all day, shadowing you through the hallway, you don't want them to be like . . . "Oh my God, get away from me!" I think you have to have more of a friend relationship there. You are with them *all* day. It is going to be a really long day if you don't have any kind of fun relationship.

Toia

So, as an interpreter, what I try to do is to allow the hearing students in the class to interact. I try to encourage interaction between the deaf students and hearing students, so the deaf student feels more relaxed and confident in that setting. But most of the time, they keep coming back and falling on the interpreter, because they have a need to communicate with someone that can communicate fluently in their language—it is just not there with the hearing students.

Most of the time the deaf student is dependent on me because they feel as though they are lost without the interpreter providing that communication. They are in a minority in a school setting, and whenever there is someone who speaks my language and understands my culture, I'm going to gravitate to that person. And I feel that is what is happening to the deaf student in the hearing school.

Mary

Even though we are taught that interpreters are not supposed to be kids' best friend, you do become their friends. They tell you about what is going on at home. They tell you about everything. Then you tell them about what you hear. You are, like, gossiping about what's happening in the school. Why? Because no one talks to them. There are times I think, "Maybe I shouldn't be that friendly," but so many times it is just you and that student; there is no one else for them to talk to.

The interpreters who engaged in more friendship-based relationships with deaf students strongly believed it is serving the student's best interest. They often recognize that the deaf/hearing peer relationships are often frustrating and unfulfilling for deaf students. These interpreters also tend to be more involved in creating bridges between the deaf students and their peers through conversations and relationship building.

The interpreters who are more friendship oriented also tend to initially see the deaf students as language deprived, alienated, and lonely. They believe that a friendship-based relationship will better serve both their personal and academic needs. Interestingly, most of these interpreters serve only one deaf student in a large school.

In the freelance world of interpreting for adults, the characteristics of a communication facilitator may be more appropriate. While deaf adults may want to feel that interpreters are their ally, they do not want an interpreter to be involved in building social bridges for them. Since most interpreter training programs train interpreters for freelance work, it would seem likely that the focus of their training has been on being a communication facilitator. But in the educational interpreting field, interpreters express varying opinions on how deeply they should be involved with students (see Figure 8.2).

Interestingly, the deaf students expressed a very strong consensus of opinion. They preferred interpreters to be friendship oriented and aligned with them. They believed that this was the most effective interpreting

Strictly engages only in communication facilitation	Engages in effective interpreting	Engages in effective interpreting
Does not engage in onversations with student/client	Chats or jokes with deaf students when appropriate	Chats or jokes with deaf students when appropriate
	Is often focused on looking and acting in a professional manner	Often engaged in building social bridges between deaf students and others
Is aligned more with hearing adults than with the deaf student		Is aligned more with the deaf student than with the hearing adults

Aligned with hearing adults   *Aligned with deaf students*

Figure 8.2   Orientation of Interpreters

model for them. As the clients, it would seem that their opinion should be heavily considered.

Relating on an Adult Level

Mary

Even in this one school, where the deaf ed. teacher signed pretty good, it still is just you and them, you and them. It is like the deaf student gets used to being with you on your level. When you go get a Pop Tart, they will say, "Will you get me one too?" None of the hearing kids are getting a pop tart, but I guess they are used to that.

Patricia

They realize the importance of your presence there. And good or bad, it can sometimes end up a love-hate relationship. They know that they need you there, but they hate that they need you there, as well.

When deaf students become accustomed to an adult as their primary communicative partner, they may begin to see themselves as part of the adult culture of the school, rather than a part of the student culture. As noted in the student responses, it seems some students learn to use their special circumstances in their favor.

The Importance of Appearance

Patricia

Do deaf students care about how I look? Oh definitely, especially the middle school students are the worst with that, or the best, whichever way you want to look at it. Ha! They are going to tell you if your hair is out of place, or if your clothes aren't matching that day, you are going to know about it, that is for sure. I think it is because we are somewhat of an extension, because they realize the importance of your presence there.

Kelly

Like students ask me, "Why are you wearing dark clothes? Why black all the time?" I explained that because I am an interpreter, I need to dress like an interpreter. I have light skin, so I must wear contrasting clothes, so you can see me easier. "Well, the other interpreters wear *cool* clothes. I like them better."

As mentioned in previous sections, deaf students view the interpreter as an extension of themselves. This theme emerges in their strong opinions of interpreter's clothing, hairstyle, and mannerisms. Julie's response is a prime example: "They can't be stuck up or be such a nit-picking professional. They need to have a normal body type, not way over weight. They need to have a cool personality. . . . My interpreter needs to have a similar personality, to kind of act like me. That's real important." However, for interpreters with a strong orientation to professionalism, it seems perplexing and frustrating that the students do not understand their need to dress professionally.

Interpreter-Student Conversation Topics

Toia

The deaf students generally talk to me about everything: their home life, their social life, which boys or girls they like in school. They basically talk to me about everything.

Kimberly

I think with all the kids I have worked with—I always tried to have a joking, teasing, have-fun attitude. Even with the [multi-handicapped] girl. We would sit around and joke and laugh, because I feel like my job is really boring, and I don't want to get up and go to work every day if I'm going to sit there in a chair and sign all day and not talk to anyone. I think if you have an outgoing personality, the hearing teacher sees how much fun you have with your student. And it makes building a relationship with them a lot easier, too. So if you are an outgoing, friendly person, they're going to be more welcoming to you in their classroom. Whereas, if you sit there as a stiff and just interpret, it is going to a much colder environment for the mainstream teacher, for the student, and for you. So, you try not to cross the line too much, but at the same time, I like getting up and going to work in the morning. Once I'm here, I am glad to be here. But I believe who I am, and my personality affects other people. So you have to be a little more outgoing and fun.

Mary
It is hard because you want to stand back like the teachers who say, "I don't want to hear about your home life," but I am hearing about their home life. The deaf students talk to me about everything. They tell me about their friends, who is a lesbian and who isn't. I'm like, "Oh no." They will say, "My mom doesn't know, but we went out here and did . . . " I'm thinking, I don't know if I should be hearing all of this. You don't ask, and you don't see it coming. But they just come up to you and tell you all of this stuff. It is hard for the kids. They don't see it. They only see they are alone.

The vignettes "Personal Confidante" and "The Substitute" further illustrate the close relationship that can develop between interpreters and deaf students.

"Personal Confidante"

My student had a problem. We went to the nurse's office. She was telling me all about her sexual problems. I'm like . . . "I don't know if I want to know this stuff." She was having a bleeding problem and passed tissue. The parent said that it is normal when you are on birth control. I'm thinking, if she was my daughter, I would be taking her to the doctor. She told me, "It is from my ex—he gave me a cyst." I'm thinking this does not sound normal, but I can't really tell her that. But again, how many parents are uneducated. I start worrying that there is something serious happening with her.

—Mary

"The Substitute"

When I was out one day, there was a sub who came in for me that day. I think she was fairly young interpreter, but she just wasn't prepared for how the girls react to the deaf education teacher and I. The girls will talk to us as if we were their girlfriends. They might say things to us that they may not necessarily say to another teacher.

Continued

But anyway, when I came back the next day, all I heard was "This interpreter just sat there. She did not even talk to us!" One girl said, "I asked her all kinds of questions . . . I asked her if she had a boyfriend, and all kinds of stuff. She looked at me like I had three heads!"

I thought to myself, "Oh my, can you imagine if my deaf student had to be with this sub interpreter the entire year!"

So see, I definitely think that that is important!

—Kimberly

Overall, it seems evident that the deaf students share intimate and personal details with their interpreters. It also seems that the interpreters begin to feel close to the deaf students and often develop a caring relationship with them. In the case of deaf students who do not have any communication at home, the interpreters can become pseudo-parents for the deaf student. This is seen in Mary's concern for her deaf student's health. While some interpreters embrace this kind of relationship, others tend to discourage it and lead the deaf students to a hearing professional who can strictly answer their questions. This distinction is at the heart of the professional vs. the friendship-oriented interpreter.

Effectiveness of Deaf Education Teachers

Interpreters often work hand in hand with deaf education teachers. In the following responses, they share the general strengths and weaknesses they have witnessed from this close association.

Patricia

I think that something is definitely lacking in the education of teachers of the deaf when they are going through school. I don't know that they are being taught properly how to work with interpreters and that in making the interpreter their best friend they can enhance the environment for the students. It is so important to the education of that child who will quickly sense tension when it exists. I have been in situations where I've had a wonderful relationship with the teacher of the deaf. It made it so much easier to get up and go to work every day. It made it so much nicer for the students, to see that we had this great rapport. To be honest, it was with teachers that had the least ability to sign well. The less ability they had to sign, the more they respected the interpreter, because they knew how valuable you were to that student's education, and to them. You were invaluable to them. However, there were some teachers who were very threatened that you were this other person in the building that knew sign language as well as them. And, that made it threatening to them. When respect is not stemming from the teacher of the deaf, you can forget about earning it from the rest of the staff in that building. If they don't regard you as a fellow professional in that building, you are going to have a very difficult school year.

Kimberly

That was the first thing that actually shocked me when I got my first interpreting job after college. She was the first deaf ed. teacher I worked with. When someone said to me "The deaf ed. teacher doesn't sign." I said, "*What?*" It had never occurred to me that a deaf education teacher wouldn't sign. I had no idea that it wasn't a requirement, or that it would even happen.

Kelly

I know one teacher that is really good is supporting and accommodating for deaf kids. But most teachers that I have seen only deal with the kids in their class-room—and only for whatever subject they are in there for. They are not really involved with supporting the deaf kids' social experiences or supporting them in coursework from their mainstream classes. It is more like, "I'm just here for the deaf kids' educational need." It's like, "OK, we aren't going to talk about math, 'cause you do that in another class."

Or the opposite happens. There is this one kid who comes into the resource room and says, "This map . . . I don't understand." The teacher says, "OK, I'll do it for you or we'll do it together." But that is not making the kids think for them-selves. So that reinforces the cycle [of low expectations] that "If I don't get it, I'm just deaf."

In this field, I think it is all about standards. People get so lax in "It doesn't matter." In every area people are just saying, "Just do it the easy way." Well, doing it the easy way, is making people graduate at the third-grade level. There needs to be stricter guidelines. Most people have such a low standard. I think the standard for deaf ed. teachers and interpreters needs to be raised significantly. There is noth-ing there for deaf education teachers [in regards to sign proficiency requirements]. *Nothing!* It is so sad! In my experience the majority of the teachers taught them-selves. They have had no formal training. They have gone to a deaf ed. program, and got their BA in deaf education, but their deaf ed., program had *no* sign lan-guage requirements. It was on their own shoulders to learn. And I hear this more and more and it *scares* me.

Toia

Their signing skills are pretty lousy. I just don't see how someone could be teaching a deaf child without the ability to sign fluently. Because, most of them graduate from a university or teacher program and have no signing skills, or just very basic skills. I feel their skills are often very poor, so they bring this kind of communication to the deaf student. And they are seen as the authority on the deaf student's education, and yet they can't communicate with the student. It is the interpreter who communicates with the deaf student. I think it is just very lousy.

Mary

When you ask any of the deaf education teachers how bad is the students hearing, they don't know. The majority doesn't know what the kids' hearing loss is. They don't know how much they are hearing, and if they read sign. They don't know. My student has a hearing support teacher, who was supposed to come today, the last period, and didn't show up.

I'm not sure . . . if you are a deaf educator, what are you really taught when it comes to deafness? I don't think they really know deaf culture. I don't think they understand certain things . . . and that is really being kind.

What is important for deaf education teachers? They need to be fluent in sign language—more than just one class. And know about deaf culture by spending time with deaf adults. As far as the deaf education teachers, some of the younger ones are more skilled. The older ones say things like, "I had a sign language class 25 years ago." And I can see it. And when the deaf student comes in, they are saying, "Do you have any problems?" [the student responds] "No" And the deaf ed. teacher just says, "OK" That is their hour with their deaf ed. teacher. Well you know kids. If they think they don't have to work, they will just say nothing is wrong, and say they don't need help, so that they can do whatever they want to do. I think it is frustrating to the student. They have to adapt, and always try to explain themselves to someone who doesn't know their language. It is just easier to say, "No, nothing is wrong."

Laurie

I think I am in the ideal place, because the teacher of the deaf also serves as an interpreter, so she knows what we face in the classroom, and understands it, and is an awesome person in communication, no matter what it is.

Cheryl

All of our deaf ed. teachers are great. They've been working in the field of deafness [over 25 years]. Well, we have one that is younger and she taught sign language to the staff after school, and she is really great. She fought hard to start ASL as a foreign language,

Jean

Candidates wishing to go into the teaching field should have some courses in deaf culture, techniques of educating the deaf child, most of all working with an interpreter.

In discussing deaf education teachers, the prevalent concerns running through the interpreters' responses were a concern for the lack of signing skill, gaps in education, lack of effort, and a need for mutual respect. While some interpreters gave positive remarks concerning their deaf education teachers' abilities, others noted severe deficiencies. Several interpreters mentioned the lack of signing skill in deaf education teachers. It seemed that the teacher's lack of skill placed a greater burden on the interpreter, while leaving the interpreter as the child's sole communication partner. It also left them feeling largely responsible for their education. The interpreters were also concerned about the knowledge gaps they perceived in some of the deaf education teachers with whom they had worked. Not only did teachers not know basic information about their own deaf students, they also did not understand deaf culture and how to work with an interpreter. Interpreters also noted a lack of effort and a need for mutual respect. Overall, from the perspectives of the interpreters, it seemed that some deaf education teachers have severe deficiencies, producing a negative impact on the learning of deaf students.

The role of the deaf education teacher is critical to the success of deaf students. Specialized knowledge in the language, learning, and the social needs of deaf students is essential in creating a positive and accessible learning environment for these students. Without these key components in place, a gap would certainly exist—to the detriment of deaf students.

Effectiveness of Regular Education Teachers

Interpreters have a close-up view of the regular education teachers' concerns, beliefs, relationship-building skills, and teaching actions with their deaf students. I ask the interpreters to tell me their observations of how regular education teachers interact with and teach their deaf students.

Patricia

I know there was one teacher that I worked with, a regular ed. teacher. She was told at the beginning of the summer that she was going to have this certain deaf child in her classroom the following year. She said she fretted about it for the entire summer. She was very nervous about where I was going to sit. That same teacher had such a pleasant experience that she asked that future deaf students always be placed in her room.

I also really think it is the interpreter's responsibility to kind of put them at ease, and let them know that it is their classroom. That is the number one thing that we need to do. Make sure that we are not referring to the student as "my student." It is not "my student"; it is "their student." Just that pronoun difference is so important for the teacher to realize that we are not sitting there in this little bubble, the deaf student and I, and then there is everybody else outside of that bubble. It is really important to always reinforce that it is their student.

Kimberly

Sometimes at the beginning of the year, I go into the regular ed. classroom and think to myself, "Oh God, it is going to be a long year." However, many times they end up being the teachers that add a little bit of fun, or actually like to joke with us. I know the social studies teacher we work with this year; he is a good teacher, no matter what the kids say. He is the one who has learned the sign for "whatever" and goes up to the deaf student and jokingly signs "whatever" all the time. It is fun. I have seen other teachers that are not that open. . . . But other than that, there are just isn't a whole lot of interaction from others in the building, unless it is a teacher that actually works with us. The foreign language people like us this year, because they think, "Oh signing, a different language."

Kelly

Some teachers are really short with the kids. The kids will say, "I need help, I don't understand." The teacher says, "Well, it's right there. I don't understand what your problem is . . . just read it." The student says, "Well, I've read it. And I still don't understand." And the teacher says, "Well just go ask someone." Well they have no one to ask. They can't sit quietly beside someone and say, "Can you explain this to me?" Then they will get all shy.

Mary

One English teacher required kids to get up in front of class and present. Well, this one deaf student doesn't voice very well. Her voice made her feel awkward. The teacher was saying, "Come on, you can do it! You can do it!" It's like they think they are just shy, when they don't realize how embarrassing it is to stand up and talk in front of the class [when you struggle with speech]. It is really hard. I think there is just a lack of education.

Toia

I see that a teacher generally teaches according to his or her culture. And, for the hearing teacher, he or she will teach to fit the needs of his or her student. As a deaf student, whenever you are in a hearing world, deaf culture is not necessarily a part of the hearing child's experience. But for the deaf child, they have to function in two cultures. It is a tough place. Once I heard a teacher ask a student "What month of the year sounds like a goat?" That is not parts of the deaf student's experience, so he or she would have no idea as to how to answer the question. They have never heard a goat.

Cheryl

It is exciting to see teachers work directly with the deaf kids, to talk one-on-one. Yell at them, tell them jokes, just like they do everyone else in their class. To me that is very rewarding, to get to that place where the teachers can do that, because it is not that way at the beginning. Or an older teacher, that you put a deaf student with, and they don't want to change, but it is exciting when you see teachers adapting. They'll ask me, "How did that go?" I'll say, "Well, if you are going to talk while [writing] the notes are on the board, then that is really hard for the deaf kid. They either need that notetaker, or let them copy the notes and then explain it. That would work so much better for them." They'll say, "OK, sure I'll do it. That's better for the other kids too." Actually, we set that up in the fall, [but they forget]. I'll say, "Remember you were going to let them copy before you start talking." They'll reply, "Oh, that's right. Remind me."

But, it's also so exciting to see staff learn sign language. Last year, for two years, we had a deaf education teacher in our school teach ASL 1, ASL 2, and I think ASL 3 & 4. And, ten teachers stayed one night every week, for three hours each night. They paid for their own books, their curriculum, and they were willing to do that. One of our administrators also joined the class. I think that is exciting when the staff wants to learn and try to communicate on their own with the deaf kids.

Cathy

We've had a program for the hearing impaired in this district for 30 years, and most of the teachers are real comfortable having our students in their room—which is good. I did run into one teacher who was really scared stiff, shaking the first day . . . physically shaking. This was a tenured teacher, too. We were just real low-key, and after every class, I would say, "That was great, I think she understood it." I think it is OK now, but it took a lot of work to get this person to relax and realize that they could pretty much teach the way they had always taught, and I would make the adjustment as the interpreter, and so forth.

Laurie

I think that the hearing teachers here make the effort to be accommodating for students. They are great. On the other hand, [sometimes] you go in and they are getting ready to show videotape. You say, "Is that closed captioned?" and they say "Uh, Oh, I forgot."

Jean

The teacher in a hearing classroom is totally dependent upon the interpreter to communicate everything that is being taught and said. Sometimes they make you feel very much a part of the educational team. Then there are others who feel threatened with you being in the room.

Linda
One of the hardest things for me is when the teacher makes a mistake. But then you think, "Wait a minute, all of the other students heard that there are 15 quarts in a gallon." So that is what they think, so why should I be telling the deaf student any different? Some teachers are OK with you bringing it to their attention and then they are happy to correct it. But other teachers don't want to hear about it.

The interpreters had a lot to say about how regular education teachers build or tear down their relationships with deaf students. Some of the positive regular education teachers are very positive, and they find ways to communicate directly with deaf students, even if it means taking extra classes or just learning a few fun signs. The effective regular education teachers remember to accommodate for deaf students and build positive relationships with interpreters and the students. Cheryl's example of teachers and administrators taking sign classes was an encouraging sign of acceptance and accommodating the needs of deaf students.

While some interpreters shared very positive feelings toward the regular education teachers, others were concerned that the teachers do not meet the needs of deaf students. These interpreters gave examples of ways that some teachers do not support deaf student learning. Their comments revealed the following themes: nervousness, lack of cultural understanding, shunning of teacher role, and lack of follow through in accommodations.

Several interpreters noticed the level of nervousness that hearing teachers felt when confronted with having deaf students in their class. Others gave chilling examples of regular education teachers refusing to *teach* deaf students—instead telling them to ask a peer for explanation. Interpreters believed that some teachers felt threatened by their presence, and therefore created a colder environment for them (see Jean's story). Also, regular

---

"The Teacher Who Hated Interpreters"

One teacher wouldn't let me into the room to interpret for the deaf students. She felt threatened with me in the room. I contacted my supervisor and administrator. They pulled the IEPs, finding it said an interpreter must be in the classroom, then my supervisor made an appointment to come by to talk with the teacher. Come to find out . . . this teacher doesn't like interpreters at all.

—Jean

education teachers often forgot to follow through with accommodation policies, requiring the interpreter to remind them again and again. Others noted a lack of ownership. Interpreters tried to correct this by constantly referring to the students as "*your* student." Interestingly, these comments also showed the extent to which interpreters are involved in daily advocacy and cultural mediation between deaf students and their hearing teachers.

These factors influence the learning and academic achievement of deaf students to a great extent. Empirical evidence dating all the way back to the "Coleman Report" (1966) has shown the tremendous effect of teacher quality on student achievement. It may take years for students to catch up after having one year with a poor teacher, and lower-achieving students are more significantly affected by teacher quality (Goldhaber & Anthony, 2004). In fact, many experts consider teacher quality as the most important school-related factor influencing student achievement (Rice, 2003). In light of this understanding, it is seems certain that the academic achievement of deaf students is clearly at risk when placed with a regular education teacher who never understands, nor accommodates for their needs. Kimberly's story is just one example of how an insensitive teacher can affect a student.

"The Culturally Incompetent Teacher"

I worked with a boy who was hard of hearing. He had the phonic ear system, where the teacher wears the microphone, and the student has the behind the ear part.

So, I thought from the beginning that this teacher might make it a long year for us. (You know how some teachers are just more welcoming than other teachers.)

This teacher would actually would go out into the hallway and make noises into the microphone to see if the student would respond to it. He would tell the other kids, "If you have noise makers at home, bring them in. We'll see if he can hear them or not!"

This student was already very paranoid anyway. He didn't need any more attention being brought to him. And someone actually brought in a whistle or something of that nature. This teacher would take it out in the hallway and then run back in and say, "Did he hear it? Did he hear it?" I'm like . . . "You don't get it?"

Continued

The student tried to laugh it off, and rolled his eyes, but you could tell it was hard for him. He was shy to begin with.

Also, this same student had pretty good speech. But, every once in a while he would stumble on a word, and it would come out different. This teacher actually once told him, "You sound like Elmer Fudd!" The student didn't bring this to anyone's attention, but I'm the one who went back into the [deaf ed.] room and said, "You will never believe what happened today!"

—Kimberly

Equality in the Classroom

Are deaf students seen as equals in the classroom? Do regular education teachers call on them and challenge them to the same degree as their hearing counterparts?

Kimberly

Sometimes teachers play a review game. Usually, I'll go up and say, "Can I see the question first, before you ask them—just so I can process it in my head quickly?" And I've had teachers say, "Hold on, let me find an easy one." I want to ask, "Are you trying to help me or is that because you think the deaf student won't be able to answer the harder questions?"

I also see them call on other kids, just to make sure they are paying attention, but they don't call on the deaf student. Maybe it is because they think that I am there and I'm handling it.

Toia

I have noticed that the hearing teachers do not generally call on the deaf students in the class. And that is for . . . I'd say 98% of the settings I have interpreted in, the teacher never calls on the deaf student.

I tend to believe that the teacher sees the deaf child as less capable in the classroom. Most of the times they are condescending when it comes to communicating with them in the classroom.

Linda

In some rooms, there isn't any difference. They are not the "poor little deaf child in the corner . . . I'll just let them do what they want." But, some teachers do treat them differently. It's like they think, "Well, she's deaf, and she's not going to get this." Well I say, "Try her! She might! You might be surprised."

If I'm the deaf child and I'm scribbling on my paper, and I see the kid next to me gets his paper thrown away because he is scribbling, what do I say. . . . Yahoo! I think some teachers let the deaf kids get away with more things. They think because he is deaf, he didn't know. I say, "He knew." It continues on later into their life.

I think, though, that with our kids being here in the mainstream, rather than at the school for the deaf, more and more people are starting to understand that they are just the same as them.

Cheryl
Individually, most of the teachers I work with, because of advocating, ask the deaf kids the same kind of questions that they ask the hearing kids. But, there are times when they let the deaf kids slide when they don't know the answer. So, sometimes they do have more pity on the deaf kids. Sometimes after class I'll say, "Would you accept that from anyone else? Well, that's your decision, it's your class."

Cathy
They tend to not call on the hearing impaired student as much as the hearing kids. But I have had some real go-getters who raise their hand, and then they do get called on. But most of the hearing impaired kids don't raise their hands or answer very often either; it is a two way street, but the teachers do tend to hesitate to call on the hearing impaired student.

Laurie
The speech teacher does push-ins, so that is a good reminder for the teacher to remember, "I need to call on the student so that the speech teacher can have some time to hear how they interact in the classroom." I think they do try to call on them, but if they do not, it is not because the child is deaf. Instead, it is because they don't call on some of the hearing students as much, either. They are not singling them out because they are deaf.

The twisted merger of low expectations and oppression seems to weave through the perspectives of interpreters when discussing equality in the classroom. Some interpreters believe that low expectations are a form of oppression, while others seem to see it as an unfair benefit to the deaf student. Either way, it seems to clearly indicate a negative influence on the education of deaf students.

How are low expectations manifested in the classroom? They emerge when teachers do not hold deaf students accountable for their work and learning. They appear when teachers treat deaf students' behavior with more leniency and excuse students from activities. Finally, low expectations can be seen in the over-accommodating that occurs for deaf students. In all of these situations, regular education teachers are communicating to deaf students that they are neither capable nor worthy of a full effort; and that their education is less important than the hearing students'.

"Low Expectations or Accommodating?"

The teachers think "this poor little deaf child, they can't do it", and they modify these tests. They just change the test to help them pass. If they have a multiple choice test, they will cross out two choices, leaving only two to choose from. They don't have to study, just guess between the two choices.

One student never did his homework, because he knew that the next day no one would make him accountable for it. The teacher would say, "OK, you have two more days to do it." Two days later, it never got done. The teachers are afraid to hold them accountable for some reason.

—Mary

"You're Deaf? No Gym."

One student is a senior this year. He doesn't take gym. He says, "I'm deaf, I don't take gym." I said, "How come the other kids have to change their clothes?" The teacher tells [the deaf kid], "You don't have to do anything if you are moving around with your friends." Of course, he doesn't have any friends. He just plays with his Sidekick the whole time during class.

I've had another student who had a Sidekick, who sat there and played with it all during class. The teacher didn't have a clue to what it was. The teachers think they are not bothering anybody. That same teacher told a hearing student that he could go ahead and use his cell phone to talk back and forth to others in the class and help each other with homework during class discussion. Well, a little bit of that might have been OK, but a lot of what was going back and forth between those phones was not schoolwork.

—Mary

The deaf student participants also confirmed the presence of low expectations in their school. They discussed their struggle with teachers and peers who expected less of them. They also shared their embarrassment and feelings of guilt by the amount of accommodation that was made for them. However, some of them called it by another name: cheating. Here is an example of one student's comments:

My interpreter and deaf ed. teacher seem to do more "spoon feeding" like I'm a baby. They take care of tests and make it easy to pass tests. I was supposed to have math in the fall, and I never learned math; they just passed me anyway. They never really taught me how to do math. I don't have homework or really have to learn anything. My teacher does all my homework for me, I never have to.

Overall, it is clear that the deaf students and the interpreters are aware of teachers' low expectations, and the students' lack of power and inferior treatment.

Interaction Between Deaf Students and Other Adults in the School

What is the nature of the interaction between the deaf students and the other adults in the building? Do they communicate directly, or with an interpreter as the intermediary?

Toia

One deaf student wanted me to go to lunch with her and order her lunch for her. As an interpreter, I told her that part of being integrated into society is that you are in a hearing setting, there are times you have to communicate without an interpreter. So if you go to the cafeteria and there is a menu on the board, you can write on paper what you would like to order, or you can point to it. That is one of the ways they try to communicate. Sometimes they try to mouth what they want.

Jean

Often times the staff in the school building will always have positive things to say about the deaf student—especially if he/she is a "good" student (not getting into trouble, completing assignments, and etc.). Usually if the interpreter isn't available the deaf student will initiate the conversation by writing down the request or question then the staff in turn will write their response. Sometimes conversation maybe just a greeting "Hi, how are you?" "How's your Mom?" or "Are you doing OK?" The interaction may be a little different than with a hearing student due to lack of communication skills—sign language and etc. on the part of the school staff.

Kelly

Some people go and take a sign class and learn "Ball . . . cat" and then come in and think they are on the same level as us.

From the responses of interpreters, it seems that the other adults in the building are generally friendly and open to communicating with the deaf student. But when communication does occur, it takes place mostly through pointing, gesturing, and writing. However, some deaf students also try to move their mouth to visually form a word, so that the hearing person can guess what they need. All of these forms of communication are mimicking what often happens out in the world as deaf people interact with the larger hearing community. Interpreters who encourage students to be flexible in advocating for their needs are teaching them a lifelong skill. Although it seems reasonable to address these skills in non-academic situations, such as the cafeteria, it is also important to remember that those areas may cause the most embarrassment for students as they struggle to communicate in front of their hearing peers.

An Analysis of the Interpreters Collective Responses

Overall, several strong themes emerged as the interpreter participants discussed their experiences with deaf students in integrated schools. A lack of communicative partners and prevailing social isolation surfaced as two prevailing concerns of interpreters for their deaf students. Even with the interpreter, the deaf student's only direct communication partner, they were often discouraged from having friendly conversations but instead were reminded to stay focused on their academic work. Interpreters described the communication among the deaf students and their hearing peers as being shallow—mostly relying on a gesture and pointing system. The topics of conversation between deaf students and their hearing peers was limited to the topic of school, rather than the typical topics discussed in exclusively hearing peer groups. The signing deaf students corroborated the interpreters' observation that an impoverished language environment existed in integrated classrooms.

Many of the interpreters believed that deaf students did not have access to the social networks present in the school. Though hearing students were most often polite to them, they rarely attempted to build friendships with the deaf students. The interpreters observed that signing deaf students were often limited to building friendships with students who chose to learn sign language. The same deaf students exhibited a tremendous amount of patience in teaching one or two friends their language. When their friends did become fluent, the deaf student lacked power in those relationships—for fear of losing their only friend. The interpreters revealed that deaf high school students were not asked out for dates, and often did not interact with their hearing peers outside of school hours.

The themes of inferiority and lack of power are also found in the observations of deaf students. Interpreters noted that both regular education teachers and the hearing students seemed to lack an understanding of the interpreting process. They would use phrases such as "Tell her" instead of speaking directly to the deaf student. It was believed that this misconception further led to an emotional distance between deaf students and their teachers and peers, as well as indicating a lack of ownership of the deaf student—all indicators of social deprivation. The experiences of the signing deaf students and deaf adult participants also supported the notion that there is a lack of social interaction in the integrated environments of deaf students.

Interpreters also expressed grave concerns about the ability of deaf students to access an interpreted education and felt that regular education teachers often had lower expectations for them. In many cases, the blame for the communication barrier was placed on the deaf student. Teachers would require the deaf students to adapt to the classroom, rather than having the classroom adapt to the deaf students' needs. Often hearing peers and teachers made deaf students feel inferior and did not give them the support necessary to succeed. The barriers to student success included unqualified interpreters, unqualified interpreter substitutes, deaf education teachers that cannot communicate fluently in ASL, and teachers who do not accommodate for deaf students' needs.

Though many interpreters felt that speaking deaf students were more easily integrated into the social network of the school, other interpreters still believed that these students were rarely accepted by their hearing peers. They were described as sitting on the fence and "trying so hard to appear hearing, while never quite being fully successful." In all, though, it seemed that the speaking deaf students had more choices in friendships and more interactive communication with their hearing peers and teachers.

When the professional/friends distinction was discussed, a divide of opinion became evident. Some interpreters felt strongly that interpreters should be more aligned with the hearing adults, thus serving in a professional interpreter role. Others saw the need to develop a closer friendship relationship with the student and become active in building social bridges between the deaf students and their hearing peers. These interpreters seemed to understand the need for deaf students to have an ally in a lonely and isolated environment. Interestingly, the deaf student participants seemed to clearly prefer interpreters who were more aligned with the friendship orientation.

Interviews With Deaf Education Teachers 9

THROUGH THE VOICES OF DEAF CHILDREN, we recognize a lack of communication access and social integration. The perspectives of the interpreters and deaf education teachers provide further insight into this issue.

Originally, the two deaf education teachers had been included as interpreter participants, since they both have experience interpreting in the classroom. However, during their interviews it was clear that their insight was distinctly different from that of the interpreters. So, it seemed relevant to present their perspectives separately.

The two deaf education teacher participants, Naomi and Suzanne, have some common elements in their background. Both teachers have master's degrees in deaf education. Both teachers have more than 8 years of experience working with deaf students in integrated classrooms. They are fluent in American Sign Language and have had prior experience teaching at residential schools for the deaf. Lastly, both teachers are currently employed in large suburban school districts supporting deaf students in resource rooms and mainstream classes.

Naomi is currently managing the education of 10 children at an elementary school. Most of her students are hard of hearing, with similar characteristics to the "speaking deaf students" described earlier in chapter 7. Suzanne serves an entire district but is primarily responsible for managing the education of the one signing deaf high school student. Both teachers have experience working with deaf students at the elementary, middle school, and high school level.

While the teachers seemed to largely agree in many areas, they also demonstrated divergent perspectives on their opinions of the value of integrated education. Their insight is valuable in that deaf education teachers often hold tremendous power in designing the deaf student's schedule, curriculum, and level of integration. In some cases, the deaf education teacher also assigns the interpreters to students.

Unlike earlier sections, Naomi's and Suzanne's comments will be presented in narrative form. An analysis follows each teacher's response.

Suzanne

I have been in situations where it [inclusion] hasn't worked well. Deaf kids have been frustrated, lonely, especially as they grow older—hit puberty—in the middle school and the high school, where you see real friendships and bonding. Students didn't necessarily have the academic skills to keep up with the pace and reading.

I'm sure I can speak to any kids in the middle school and high school. Even hearing kids have a hard time with their own identity: who they are and what they want to become. So I would think there is even a tougher challenge placed on the deaf child. They are obviously so different, and they feel bad, and at this stage in their life, most of them do not want to be different. So, it would be very difficult.

Numbers help. If there is any way to increase numbers. Then put your strongest staff out there. You hire someone who interacts well with the teachers. There is just a lot of education that has to happen in the school. Anything they can do to enrich the use of sign language. Every school should offer American Sign Language as a foreign language. It is recognized in so many states now. That would be a huge benefit. Flexibility in scheduling, curriculum-wise, putting friends in classes. Scheduling so that if students wanted to go half time to a deaf ed. program, or some kind of outreach from the residential school, they can do that.

I also think it is important to engage the deaf students. Deaf students should learn to advocate for themselves in the public school setting. They should meet with their teachers and explain about their deafness and the role of interpreters, etc. This gives them ownership in their learning. In [my previous state] student-led IEPs were really being promoted. The special ed. teacher worked with the high school students to plan their own goals, objectives, etc. and then the student led his/her own IEP. It was great for building the student's ownership of their learning environment.

A lot of the older teachers started as oralists, and then we had the whole Signed English craze. And some people are just not good at foreign languages. But, there was always this mentality that if you worked with little kids, you didn't need to sign well. As a boss, I can't even fathom hiring someone that would have to go through an interpreter to work with the student. And, I'm a very strong believer in that if you are fluent in American Sign Language, you can adapt and sign more English. But, it doesn't work the other way around. But, I can understand the kids' frustration.

Deaf ed. is a different ballgame. You are the person the student talks to. You are the person [from whom they] learn about behavior. We do a lot of pragmatic things, like saying, "In deaf culture that is acceptable, but in the hearing culture, that is not appropriate." And to not understand both cultures, and to not be able to form that relationship with the student is hard to imagine.

You need to understand and respect their first language, American Sign Language, to teach English as a second language. I'll say, "You know how you just signed that? We don't add that in English. In sign language you say it like this, but in English you write it like this." For example, deaf kids don't know about the word "is" in sign, because it is incorporated in what you sign. I'll say, "Let me show you." If you don't have a grasp of the language, you are missing the ability to do that.

One of the biggest changes I have seen between different states and agencies is in the models and philosophies that different agencies assume for the role of the interpreter. The model that I came from was that the interpreter was strictly an interpreter, almost as an [free lance] interpreter in a professional setting following the Code of Ethics. The interpreter didn't discuss anything with the classroom teacher. They didn't engage in any friendships with the kids. Everything was refereed back to the teacher of the deaf. In some ways, that was nice, because it did build that understanding that it is my responsibility to work with the hearing teachers. But in many ways, it was so unnatural. We had kindergartners, first graders, second graders, third graders who in no way were at a developmental stage, or emotional stage where they could understand "what I say, they sign." They naturally saw this person as a friend or as a mother figure, or an adult in their life. They needed that friendship.

I've also seen at the high school level some kids needing that ability to bond. Here is finally someone who can speak fluently to me, who can talk to me about the world, who can talk about politics, and has a wealth of information to talk about. Interpreters and the deaf kids do develop close friendships. In the ideal world, I would like to think there are enough deaf kids in the classroom to develop normal friendships, and the adults in the room could develop a more personal/impersonal relationship with them.

But, that is just not "deaf culture." There is a closeness in residential schools, because you have five or six students, and you see the students grow up, and each class going through the grade levels. And there is a natural bonding . . . in deaf education, you are not just teaching English, you are teaching about the world. Many of these deaf students come from hearing parents, and there is so much more that you do than teaching reading and writing. You have to teach about the world.

So there has always been a closeness in deaf ed. It is more familial and it is different than this huge mainstream setting. So, I don't have a problem with interpreters being close to their students because I think it is an extension of this [deaf culture]. I have grown deaf adult friends who see an interpreter at a function, and they sit and chat with them. It is natural.

My experience has been that there are always limitations when we are talking about profoundly deaf students. They have their own language, which is American Sign Language, but other kids in that setting do not sign. Even those who do learn to sign, are not native signers, or near the fluency we want. So there is the fact that the interactions tend to be less in depth, less numerous. They tend to be superficial based on the hearing student's sign vocabulary, or the other alternative is that the communication has to go through an adult. That adult tends to be an interpreter, so it is not a natural setting for a student to go through school with an interpreter, and everything that is said must go through that interpreter. And everything the deaf child says comes back through the interpreter. My experience has been that most hearing students are pleasant, they are nice, in that they don't make fun of the deaf student. However, I wonder how close their relationships ever become.

At the middle school and high school level, you do get some more students who sign, and sign much better—even maybe sign very well. But, it is almost as if the friendships formed by the deaf students are left up to who learns to sign. The deaf student can't just pick any student and say, "Hey, I get along good with this person, I want to be their friend." Instead, they start relating to only the kids who learn to sign. If that person does not share their background or interest, than the only thing they do have in common is they can communicate. So that is a hindrance.

But, in order to develop fully as adults, we need to be exposed to a variety of different people, from all walks of life. All interaction can be significant, whether that be the cafeteria lady talking to you about how much is left in your account, or what you need to do in the library—just the ability to ask for a book and be able to chat. We are not sending an interpreter with them to return a library book, and they have to function in the real world.

But, it is a different experience. In some ways people will try to interact with a deaf student. The classroom teacher may warm up to them because they have exposure to them day in and day out. Different people in the building will either avoid the deaf child, or make an effort. The older the deaf child is, and the more comfortable they are in the setting makes a difference.

But again, it is superficial. They can write back and forth. They write notes, or at the cafeteria they will point to the screen, and the deaf student will give a thumbs up, if they understand. But, definitely they miss voices. I think about day-to-day announcements . . . the schools' TV news.

And, there are all of these voices every day, that come through the same person and the same filter. Any time you interpret a message, it is going through *me*, so I am putting my own bias into it. I decide what ASL slang word to use for the English slang word. Everything they hear from the other kids, from the teacher, from the lunch lady, is never coming to them directly. And it doesn't give them the opportunity to figure out for themselves "Oh, she was really mad." We make those judgments by the way we interpret it for the deaf student. If we don't feel they were mad, we don't pass that on. There is innuendo and other things that are definitely being missed.

Analysis of Suzanne's Interview

Suzanne's interview corroborates the signing deaf students' perspectives in many ways. Her recognition of the barriers that deaf students face in integrated settings echoes many themes found in the deaf student's comments; loneliness of students, lack of communication, difficulty in building relationships with hearing students, and the need for deaf students to bond with others who share their language. Her comments focus on the social needs of deaf students, and the inability of the regular ed. school to provide for those needs.

Expressions of loneliness and lack of communication were evident in many deaf student interviews. Suzanne also seemed highly aware of this struggle when she stated, "My experience has been that there are always limitations when we are talking about profoundly deaf students. They have their own language, which is American Sign Language, but other kids in that setting do not sign."

When speaking of her involvement in building support structures for deaf students, Suzanne gave general suggestions for increasing the success of deaf students: providing social support, providing educational support, and teaching students to advocate for themselves. She emphasized the benefit of having a larger number of deaf students in the school. She also noted the importance of hiring good teachers, who can positively interact with others, scheduling deaf students in classes with peers that sign, and offering ASL as a foreign language, to increase the communicative peer group of deaf students. Suzanne also indicated the need to encourage deaf students to advocate for themselves and involve them in the IEP development process.

Suzanne takes an active role in of nurturing any budding relationships between the deaf students and their peers, by regularly inviting the hearing peers to eat lunch with herself, the interpreter, and the deaf student. During lunchtime, they teach sign language and further encourage the friendship. However, the number of social relationships that develop between a deaf student and his or her hearing peers seems to be highly dependent on the personality of the deaf student and the willingness of the hearing students to find ways to communicate. This observation was also noted by the deaf students; they clearly stated the limitations that they experience in trying to build relationships with hearing students. Not only do few hearing students learn to sign, but the deaf students feel "stuck" choosing friends from only the few hearing students who do learn to sign.

In alignment with the views of many interpreters, Suzanne indicates that many deaf education teachers are not fluent in American Sign Language, and many do not even know the most basic signs to communicate. In her example, she demonstrates a need for linguistic and cultural fluency in meeting both the social needs and the academic needs of the student. She also addresses the myth that the ability to communicate through an English-based system is adequate. She strongly asserts that an understanding of ASL grammar is essential in teaching ASL to deaf students.

In her interview, Suzanne reminds interpreters of the importance of skills beyond interpreting. She recognizes that personality and collaborative social skills, both her own and those of the interpreters, are critical in serving the needs of deaf students. Again, this perspective is clearly reflected in the opinions of the deaf students interviewed.

Overall, Suzanne's perspective seems closely aligned with that of the signing deaf students. She understands the barriers that deaf students experience, and she exposes the tremendous effort that she engages in to serve their emotional, educational, and social needs. She fully believes that the success of deaf students in integrated educational settings heavily depends on this in-depth support.

Naomi

Of course it [the integrated classroom experience] is all individualized; no two deaf children are alike, just like there are no two hearing children that are alike. It all depends on the student, their comfort level in an environment with hearing peers, and it depends on their language fluency and how well they use an interpreter. If they are not comfortable using an interpreter, they are not ready to go in the classroom using an interpreter, because the learning process will be too difficult. Then it would be my job to still teach them, but also train them in how to use an interpreter before they are placed in a hearing classroom.

I guess children who are basically shy have a more difficult time. And so sometimes that takes maturity. As they get older, they break out of their shell, and then they are more comfortable in the classroom. If students are placed here when they are very young, I have to look at that as a factor, too. But, most of them don't have difficulty. Some students are shy in a sense, in that they are shy in whole, not just around hearing people, but shy around everybody. Once in a while I get students who come here after they've been in a program or a school for the deaf, and they are shy in a sense that they are so used to being with only deaf people and only people who sign all day long, then they are a little apprehensive because they are not sure of how to deal with a different culture. So we have to work on that before we place them into the classroom.

The students who thrive are the ones who are comfortable with themselves the way they are. They are the ones who have accepted the fact that they need certain ways to communicate, and they also are not afraid to express that need to their peers and their teachers. They also thrive because when they first come here we do a good job (I think we do a good job) of in-servicing everyone.

One of the keys is in-servicing everyone. If you don't in-service everybody, then that doesn't help the student with their comfort level. So not only do we in-service the staff, we also in-service the students when they come in at a young age—when they enter the school building in kindergarten, we let them know that there are other kids here that have another way of communicating. We make it part of the school. It is just part of who we are as a team here in this school building. If you want to be friends with these students, or work with them, these are the ways you need to interact. It is not something the hearing students do not understand. They have the knowledge and are not apprehensive, so that comfort level for everyone helps the students thrive. If there are any students who wither, it is because they haven't taken ownership of who they are. They haven't taken ownership of the things they need to do, to go back and forth between cultures, and to go back and forth between communication systems.

At recess time, we have an interpreter out with them, just in case our students want to play a game or communicate with one of the other students. Everyone knows that if they are having difficulty interacting with someone who uses sign language as a main mode of communication, there is always someone there who can facilitate that communication, so they can be part of each other's world.

The level of integration depends on the students. Many of them will integrate because they want to play the same games, because you need a whole group of people, you can't just play with one or two. So they will integrate, and will look to the interpreter for assistance, if they don't understand the rules that the kids have made up, or specific games. Some of the deaf students will go off by themselves—the ones who prefer doing something individualized. They will find a buddy who also signs, and they will go off by themselves, but it varies from student to student. I've seen it from one extreme to the other.

I've seen students who verbalize well not have as many friends as students who use sign language as their main mode of communication. It is the personality thing that comes into play. There are some children who sign, whose personality is so warm and wonderful, that all the kids want to be with them and will learn signs to communicate with them, where others kids may speak but are very shy, or don't think their speech is good enough, or understandable enough, and they are a little more hesitant to communicate with the hearing children. So they might back off and not have as many friends. But I've also seen the opposite. So it varies.

In my current school, the deaf students are seen as equal to hearing students, because they follow the same rules, they get the same consequences if they break the rules, they have the same tests, there is not much difference. I think it is because they have all been in-serviced on why a student comes here, and why a deaf students needs an interpreter.

I've taught students from kindergarten to high school. Now that I am teaching younger students, one of the things we try to do is to train them in how to use an interpreter. We try not to put them into the setting until they are ready. Second, we use an inverted pyramid with the students and the interpreter. When the children are very young, the interpreter's role is huge. They are not only helping the students to learn how to use the interpreter, but many times they have to take the student and teach them the signs in this (deaf ed.) classroom, before they go into the regular classroom. They have a huge role. They help the students know where to sit, so that they can see both the interpreter and the teacher. They help them to look when another student is talking. They help them to know the routine of the classroom. But as the student becomes older, all of those jobs become the student's role, and the interpreter's job becomes strictly interpreting—communication facilitation—voicing and signing. By the time they get to middle school and high school, we want them to know that that is the interpreter's role. The interpreter is there to facilitate communication for everyone in the building. They are not assigned to "you." They are assigned to the entire building. They are to facilitate communication between everyone involved in that building with you and that school.

This kind of setting has great benefits preparing students for the real world. I think if everyone involved knows what is best for each student and does what they need to do to make sure that his/her education is individualized, it can be very successful. It takes a lot of "behind the scenes" preparation and in-servicing for this to happen. It takes a team effort of committed people. And, nothing thrills me more than to get e-mails, cards, letters, or phone calls from students I taught when they were young who are now graduated from college and doing great work. They are out there enjoying their independence, their work, and their families, and loving it. It just makes it all worthwhile. I see successes every day.

Analysis of Naomi's Interview

Naomi believes that most deaf students can succeed in an integrated school as long as they are confident in who they are. She defines this as taking ownership of the things they need to do, and the ability to go back and forth between cultures and communication systems. Her positive experiences in supporting students seem to be more closely aligned with the speaking deaf students interviews.

Like Suzanne, Naomi seriously attends to building social support structures for deaf students. Naomi emphasized the importance of in-servicing the teacher in how to take ownership of the student, so that the other students will be equally inclined to take ownership of the student. But in discussing the role of the interpreter, Naomi's and Suzanne's interviews represent very different viewpoints. Naomi advocates a more distant professional relationship for interpreters by telling deaf students, "They are not assigned to 'you.' They are assigned to the entire building. They are to facilitate communication between everyone involved in that building with you and that school." She supports a diminishing role for the interpreter as the students become older.

These two teachers also disagree about the ability of deaf students to succeed in an inclusive school.

An Interpretative Summary of the Deaf Education Teachers' Responses

Overall, it seems that the two deaf education teachers have shared understanding of the role of the deaf education teacher in the following areas: providing academic support for deaf students, providing support for deaf students in their social integration, advocating for students needs, and providing in-service training for staff members. Both teachers support deaf students in their academic and social integration within the school. Both teachers advocate strongly for student needs, as well as for their time with students. Both teachers provide extensive in-service training to teachers, hearing students, and others in the building. All of these actions would seem to build strong foundations for the success of deaf students in integrated classrooms.

However, the two deaf education teachers have contrasting opinions of the role of the interpreter. Though both teachers feel strongly that interpreters should be well qualified, Naomi supports a more distant professional relationship with the interpreter, while Suzanne believes the ability of the interpreter to bond with the deaf student is critical to their success.

Naomi believes that the level of social integration is dependent on the deaf student. She feels her program has made positive contributions to the deaf students' social integration by providing interpreters at the playground to facilitate play and interaction between deaf and hearing students. But, she also recognizes the influence of a deaf student's personality on his or her ability to make friends. When deaf students do not succeed in integrated settings, Naomi places the blame for failure on the deaf students: "If there are any students who wither, it is because they haven't taken ownership of who they are. They haven't taken ownership of the things they need to do, to go back and forth between cultures, and to go back and forth between communication systems."

Suzanne, however, sees the integrated system as unable to provide adequate social stimulus and therefore incapable of promoting success for many deaf students. In her view, the system is inadequate in providing the communicative interaction needed to grow. She believes that deaf students will always be at a disadvantage in a world where they are surrounded by communication barriers. She recognizes that two problems exist in the relationships between deaf and hearing students: (1) the relationships aren't close because of the hearing students limited ability to sign, and (2) deaf students are restricted to building friendships with peers that sign. Suzanne sees both of these issues as adding to the barriers that deaf students face in their ability to have normal social experiences. When deaf students fail, she places the blame on the system:

> My experience has been that there are always limitations when we are talking about profoundly deaf students. So there is the fact that the interactions tend to be less in depth, less numerous. They tend to be superficial based on the hearing student's sign vocabulary, or the other alternative is that the communication has to go through an adult. That adult tends to be an interpreter, so it is not a natural setting for a student to go through school with an interpreter.

These two teachers think quite differently about the experiences of deaf students. They both care deeply about the success of deaf students, and they go beyond their contractual agreements to provide social support structures for deaf students. Both teachers understand the struggles that deaf students face but react to them very differently. Naomi sees the integrated educational environment as a place where, with appropriate support and teaching, deaf children can excel on the same level as hearing students. Suzanne believes the communication barriers are too great for most deaf students to overcome. Both viewpoints are profound and certainly strike at the heart of the issues under inquiry.

These two contrasting philosophies are also represented in the voices of deaf students and interpreters. Several speaking deaf students felt very happy and successful in integrated schools. And, many interpreters seem to also support Naomi's view that the current integrated educational system is capable of supporting the success of deaf students. But the deaf signing students did not hold this opinion.

When the deaf child is not successful, some interpreters also suggest that it is the child's fault. They say that the failure is due to the child's inability to watch the interpreter or to function in a bilingual and bicultural educational environment. They claim it is the child's personality that prevents him or her from making friends. In each scenario, the blame is placed on the deaf student.

Most signing deaf students and deaf adults agree with Suzanne—the system is incapable of meeting the linguistic and social needs of deaf students. They believe the system is failing to provide deaf students with sufficient opportunities to communicate, interact, and build relationships. The result is language deprivation and social isolation. These opposing underlying beliefs have led to variances in the ways that teacher relate to the students and to how they attempt to provide appropriate support systems.

Interviews With Regular Education Teachers

10

THE REGULAR EDUCATION TEACHERS INTERVIEWED all teach in large suburban districts in Pennsylvania. They have experience teaching at least one deaf student in their class with the support of an educational interpreter (see Table 10.1). They are located in separate school districts. The teachers' responses have been organized by the following topics.

- academic achievement
- meeting the needs of deaf students
- relationship with the deaf student
- accommodating for the needs of the deaf student
- relationship building between deaf and hearing students
- communication between deaf and hearing students
- working with an interpreter in the room
- support from the deaf education teacher
- advice for other teachers
- unexpected findings, and
- purpose of integration

An analysis discusses the themes that emerged within the responses. The final section presents a collective discussion of the major themes found throughout the regular education teacher interviews.

Table 10.1 Experiences of Regular Education Teachers

Teacher	Grade level			Number of years teaching deaf students
	Elementary	Middle school	High school	
Eric			X	1–3
Richard		X		4–6
Mindy	X	X		7 or more
Amy			X	1–3

169

Narrative Sketches of Regular Education Teachers

Eric: Eric has taught for eight years in a high school math department. His high school has several deaf mainstreamed students. His reflections of having a deaf student are based on his experiences last school year, before he was transferred into a new position as a school principal.

Richard: Richard has been teaching technology and computer classes for many years. He seems flexible and sensitive in meeting the needs of all students. His interview is a reflection of his recent experiences with one deaf student in his class.

Mindy: Mindy has had extensive experience with deaf students in her classroom. For several years, she taught fifth grade but is now a seventh grade math teacher. All of her experience with deaf students has occurred in the same school district. She is very outgoing and creative and has a strong desire to see kids excel.

Amy: Amy is a young high school math teacher. In her interview, she reflects upon her recent experience of having a deaf student in her class for the first time. She seems to have a reflective approach towards her teaching and thinks deeply about how to meet the needs of her one deaf student.

Academic Achievement

I asked the teachers about the deaf students' performance in class. I was especially interested in their perceptions of the deaf students' ability to understand the content at the same level as the hearing students.

Richard

I have just one [deaf student] this year, and he seems to do well, As and Bs in everything. And, he has an interpreter with him all day long.

Mindy

If they really and truly use an interpreter, as they should, their learning should not be much different at all. Not at all. Not in my experiences. If they put up their hand and say, "I didn't understand you," I know it is because they didn't watch the interpreter, and I let them know about that.

Amy

This is the first time I have ever had a deaf student. It is a totally new challenge for me, especially if I didn't have the interpreter . . . . But it does help me to completely think about "Am I doing things that are making it harder for her, easier for her?"

The teachers approached questions about academic achievement from very different angles. All teachers seemed to be concerned for the academic success of the student, yet their responses centered on different points of focus. While Richard judged the student's abilities by the outward sign of getting good grades, Amy looked inwardly to try to understand how she could help the student be more successful.

Mindy's responses reflect two myths about inclusive education. First, she believes that an interpreted education is equivalent to a direct education. However, several factors affect the quality of an interpreted education, including the student's receptive and expressive language capabilities, the interpreter's receptive and expressive language capabilities, and the interpreter's ability to process one language effectively into another language. The second myth that Mindy introduces is that it is the student's fault if they do not understand the teacher. Many researchers, however, have shown that interpreter quality is often poor (Yarger, 2001; Patrie, 1994; Jones, Clark, & Stoltz, 1997; Winston, 1994a.). Additionally, deaf students do not have access to the incidental learning of other students, and, therefore, they may need further instruction. Toia, one of the educational interpreters, mentioned this during her interview.

> Most times, the hearing child goes into a history class, and they have much background knowledge in history. They hear it all the time on television, or on the radio, or from family or friends talking about the Korean War or the Vietnam War. For the deaf child, they have no clue about what has happened because their grandparents don't sign, and their aunts and uncles don't sign. So they have no idea. I see deaf kids as at a great loss when they go into the classroom.

These factors, which are beyond the students' control, influence their learning. It is unfair to deaf students to simply place the full blame on them for not understanding.

Mindy's comment reveals a frustration that many teachers and interpreters experience—an annoyance with deaf students who will not watch the interpreter. Obviously, if deaf students are not watching the interpreter, they are not accessing the instruction in the classroom. However, not many professionals consider the strict discipline that is involved in "watching the interpreter" for hours every day. While hearing students can change their eye gaze to check their notes, handouts, and other supportive materials, the deaf students are restricted to *watching the interpreter*. But by doing so, they are cut off from the visual stimuli of the teacher's body language, posture changes, facial expression, and other points of reference. Even peer reaction to the content, which is normally available by reading others' body language, is inaccessible. It takes a great deal of discipline to disregard the other visual stimuli in the room and focus on an interpreter. And yet even very young deaf children are required to watch the interpreter in order to access their education.

If a deaf child raises his hand, admitting that he does not understand, it is unthinkable that a teacher would use this opportunity to scold the student for not watching the interpreter. Such a reprimand is likely to result in the child never raising his hand again to ask a question.

Meeting the Communication Needs of Deaf Students

In what ways do you feel you are able to meet the learning and communication needs of the deaf student in your classroom?

Eric

Um . . . I don't know. Like I said, they were just kind of there. Maybe I'm not a good one to talk to, because I really had no idea what to do with them. We just kind of went about our daily activities, and the deaf student just was there.

Richard

I think it is important to have good communication with the aide, because the aide observes a lot in how he is reacting, and how he is understanding, his feelings. I suppose I would prefer a little more feedback than I do get this year. But the person working with my special needs student does a good job. I'm glad she is there, but if I had my perfect aides, for example, I would probably wish for a little more feedback, like, "This is how things are going this week," maybe, "He's having a rough time at home," or "He's falling behind on this project, and I can tell he is nervous." You know, I usually don't get much feedback. Maybe I should ask more.

Amy

The interpreter will ask if she has a question, but hopefully, it is working out OK for her. I think for me, I try to start the year out picking out specific students [for questioning] and I get into a habit of waiting for students to volunteer. The deaf student will volunteer every now and then, but that would be a good goal for me to try to call on students. I don't think that the deaf student is called on any less, because there are a lot of students I do not call on.

When the teachers reflected on their ability to meet the needs of deaf students, they discussed communication, questioning techniques, and general feelings of having the deaf student in their class. But the emerging theme among all responses was the teachers' lack of understanding of their deaf student's level of learning. Eric speaks as though the deaf student is invisible. He says, " I really had no idea what to do with them." This would lead one to believe that teaching them was not his immediate priority. When Richard discussed his student's achievement, he states, "You know, I usually don't get much feedback. Maybe I should ask more." This comment would seem to indicate that the student belongs to the interpreter, and he would need to ask the interpreter to see if the student is learning. Amy responded, "The interpreter will ask if she has a question, but hopefully, it is working out OK for her," indicating that it is the interpreter's responsibility to monitor the deaf student's learning. In all, it seems that the regular education teachers did not have a firm understanding of the deaf students' learning needs.

Unexpectedly, another theme emerged in the teachers' responses, the theme of social exclusion. It is most clear in Eric's response when he says, "They were just kind of there . . . we just kind of went about our daily activities, and the deaf student just was there." By using the terms "we" versus "the deaf student," Eric indicates that he did not see the student as part of the class. Instead, the deaf student was considered to be outside the social realm of the class. Also, Eric reiterates "they were just there," indicating that the deaf student was present but not interacting with peers, teachers, or curriculum. In a later section, Mindy also reports, "If you have a kid who just sits there and wants everyone to wait on them, they don't have friends." Again, the assumption is that it is the deaf student's fault that they are unable to interact with their environment.

Another interesting note is that Richard used the term aide interchangeably with interpreter. He did not seem to be aware of the separate meanings of those words. Interestingly, he referred to the interpreter as one of "my aides," and he referred to the interpreting process as, "working with one of my special needs students," further indicating a lack of understanding for the role of an interpreter.

Relationship Between the Regular Education Teacher and the Deaf Student

As teachers reflected on their relationships with their deaf students, they shared the following comments:

Eric

Well, if I needed to tell the deaf student something, then I'd tell the interpreter. She'd tell her. The deaf student was just kind of there. They really didn't talk with us very much. You know, they had an interpreter to tell them everything.

Mindy

My relationship with the deaf students is really no different. I treat the hearing kids and the deaf kids the same. I treat them with the same consequences for not having homework done. So I let them know about that, too. So I don't treat them any differently.

Amy

Having a student who can't hear and having to go through an interpreter is a little bit of a barrier. But as the year has gone on, I've been trying to talk directly to the student even though the interpreter is communicating for us. I tell myself that I want to talk directly to the student, even though she will probably be looking at the interpreter. But that is one thing I've really been trying to be more conscious of. In fact, sometimes I think I have a better relationship with her than a lot of other kids. She'll come up and talk to me because she is worried that she got a poor grade on something, and she is worried that it will pull her whole grade down. Or, they will just come to talk to me when I'm free just to ask a question, so it gives me a little more time to talk to her.

What kinds of relationships do regular education teachers have with deaf students? Three very different beliefs and philosophies are represented in the responses of the regular education teachers: distance, punitive equality, and reflective relationship building. Eric's response seems to reflect a distance between himself and the deaf student. It also indicates a distance between the deaf student and the other students. While relationship building depends primarily on a sense of interaction and communication, Eric does not seem to understand the interpreting process. Typically in interpreting, the conversation is considered to be between the deaf person and the hearing person. The interpreter only serves as a facilitator for the message. But Eric says that he is has a conversation with the interpreter, who then has a conversation with the deaf student. This sense of distance is repeated again when he says, "they had an interpreter to tell them everything." Also, Eric does not seem to take responsibility for the student. He sees the deaf student as separate from himself and the rest of the class when he states, "They really didn't talk with us very much."

Mindy's response centers on equality, not relationship building. Her focus is on ensuring that the deaf student faces the same consequences as the hearing students. Although deaf students may benefit from a system of equality in the classroom, this does not lead to relationship building between them and the teacher.

Although this is Amy's first year working with a deaf student, she has a strong desire to help the student feel comfortable and welcome. She mentions her attempts to look at the deaf student when talking with her, even though the student may be looking at the interpreter. In doing so, Amy is making a direct connection with the deaf student and is simultaneously creating a closer relationship. Interestingly, Amy shares that she may be even closer to the deaf student than to other students, because she meets with her and the interpreter outside of class to ensure that the deaf student understands the content covered in class.

Relationship Building Between Deaf and Hearing Students

What is your perspective of the relationship building between deaf students and hearing students?

Eric

Hmm . . . the kids were nice to her, and all. But, you know, they couldn't sign. Well . . . some of them may have learned the alphabet. I guess it would have helped if the deaf student could have read lips better, but she tried.

Richard

He doesn't interact much with the other kids. Many times I will demonstrate some skills with a certain program, and then give an assignment where students work on a project. And during that time the kids look at each other's work and they interact, so it's not a rigid classroom. He's usually to himself. I don't know, maybe that is just his personality. He doesn't make attempts to interact with the other children, and they don't go out of their way to interact with him. I'm sure the interpreter would be willing to [interpret between him and the other students], but I don't see any of that interaction going on.

I don't know how the other students see the hearing impaired student—in terms of ability. More than likely, from the way that I treat him, I suspect that they see him as an equal. They don't say anything. They don't make fun of him. There is nothing like that.

Mindy

The deaf kids that I have had in my classes, that talk with the hearing kids, act very normal. [Some] don't talk to the other kids, like a student I have now that has absolutely no social skills—doesn't like to work in a group, doesn't like to work with anyone else, only wants to work completely alone. But other kids work very well in groups. They tend to have some speech. I think if they are profoundly deaf, and they don't have any speaking abilities, it makes it more difficult for them to socialize with the other kids. But if they are not profoundly deaf, and they even speak with impediments—they are still understandable, those kids socialize on a more hearing level, like the hearing kids do.

I think the other kids' acceptance of a deaf student is dependent on the personality of the deaf kid. If you have a deaf child who is lively, happy, and always ready to try anything new, I think those kids make friends. If you have a kid who just sits there, and wants everyone to wait on them, they don't have friends. Kids don't socialize with selfish kids. I think unfortunately, that is what happens with kids that have disabilities, because the parents have coddled them and coddled them and it makes them unreachable to normal other kids. I don't know if that is the right thing to say, but I've just seen so many different kids. Some of them have such great personalities, and they are great kids to talk to. But other kids come in and sit down, and it is like . . . Boom . . . they are just there.

Amy

She just blends right in with everyone, so often I completely forget. I think overall the hearing students are used to the deaf student. Sometimes I think that they would react a little bit more, but they are so used to it. You have a few students who would snicker a little bit, when the deaf student is laughing and makes a little different noise, or if she is trying to say something. But that is only a handful of them.

When discussing the peer interaction and relationship building between deaf students and hearing students, the following themes emerged: responsibility placed on the deaf student to adapt, the easier social integration of speaking deaf children, and a general emotional distance between the hearing students and the deaf signing students. First, many of the regular education teachers place the responsibility for communication on the deaf student. This is noted clearly in Eric's comment, "I guess it would have helped if the deaf student could have read lips better." It also seems evident in Mindy's comment, "But other kids come in and sit down, and it is like . . . Boom . . . they are just there." And, it is seen in Richard's comment, "He doesn't interact much with the other kids." While the hearing students have the ability to learn sign language to communicate with the deaf student, the deaf student may not necessarily be able to learn to read lips or speak. But curiously, some teachers place the responsibility to adapt on the deaf student.

A second theme that is continued by the regular education teachers is the notion that speaking deaf children are more easily integrated into the social network of the classroom. Mindy states, "But if they are not profoundly deaf, and they even speak with impediments—they are still understandable, those kids socialize on a more hearing level, like the hearing kids do." Since Eric, Richard, and Amy have no experience with speaking deaf students, they did not address this issue. But this theme is carried through from the responses of deaf students, deaf adults, and the interpreters.

A third theme emerging in the responses of the teachers was the emotional distance between hearing students and deaf signing students. Eric's comments were insightful: "The kids were nice to her, and all. But, you know, they couldn't sign." This notion seems to refer back to the vignette "Politeness, Not Friendship" in the interpreter section, where hearing students are polite but do not engage in relationship building. Richard indicates that the hearing students treat the deaf student as though they were invisible: "They don't say anything. They don't make fun of him." But Amy does admit that a handful of kids do make fun of her student. Overall, it seems that the regular education teachers, like the other study participants, have noticed the emotional distance between deaf students and hearing students.

Communication Between Hearing and Deaf Students

Do hearing students learn sign language? What is the nature of communication between hearing and deaf students?

Eric
[The hearing kids can't] sign. Well . . . some of them may have learned the alphabet.

Richard
I have never seen any of my students use sign language—never.

Mindy

No, not unless they are forced to. Most of them don't learn it unless there is a reason.

From the perspectives of the regular education teachers, it seems that hearing students rarely learn sign language to communicate with their deaf peers. If anything, they may learn the alphabet, but they are unable to communicate directly with deaf students. Interestingly, Mindy's comment, "Most of them don't learn it, unless there is a reason," would seem to indicate that most hearing students do not see a reason to learn sign language, even though they sit next to deaf students in class. This lack of interest further extends the emotional distance between deaf and hearing students. It also reflects the presence of language deprivation and social isolation for deaf students in regular education classrooms.

Support From the Deaf Education Teacher

In what ways does the deaf education teacher support you or accommodate or the deaf students' learning in the classroom?

Eric

I think I know the deaf ed. teacher. He used to come by the first week of class.

Mindy

Not me, because I have a special ed. degree. I've worked with deaf ed. kids for nine years and I just know what to do with them. It makes a big difference when you just forget about their differences and don't treat them any differently.

Amy

I haven't seen the deaf ed. teacher in a while. She comes in when the interpreter isn't here to substitute for the interpreter. She doesn't really do anything with me. Sometimes someone will come up and ask if the deaf student can get the test a period early, because it may take the student longer to take it, especially if there are word problems to interpret.

The collective responses indicate that deaf education teachers are rarely involved in offering support to regular education teachers or making accommodations for deaf students. Therefore, it would seem that the managing of the deaf students' education is left to a collaborative arrangement between the regular education teacher and the interpreter.

Purpose of Integration

What is the primary purpose of educating deaf students with hearing students?

Mindy
Social development! The deaf kids that I have seen have social problems, because they don't do the chit chatting that all the other kids normally do. So, they don't learn the feedback symbols that you learn in conversation. So I see the social interactions are the neediest part of most deaf children.

Mindy's reply brings up a fundamental question about inclusion: Why are deaf students placed in an environment where their communication and social opportunities are severely limited in order to improve their social skills? Mindy recognizes that the deaf students in her classroom have social problems because they "don't do the chit chatting that all the other kids normally do." She seems to understand that this deprivation serves as a barrier to their ability to learn the basic techniques of conversation, which, in turn, limits their social interactions.

Summary of Regular Education Teachers' Collective Responses

Overall, several strong themes emerged as the regular education teachers discussed their experiences with deaf students in integrated classrooms. These themes included: language deprivation and social isolation, the teachers' lack of ownership of the deaf student, a lack of education, and a willingness to accommodate student's needs.

First, regular education teachers seemed to agree that hearing students rarely learn sign language and have little interaction with deaf students. Several teachers also seemed to place the responsibility for communication on the deaf student or attribute this lack of interaction to the deaf child's personality. This perspective also emerged in the comments of the speaking deaf students, who tended to blame the communication barrier on the deaf student. The lack of communication with peers would seem to indicate a theme of language deprivation and social isolation.

Several of the teachers expressed a lack of ownership of the deaf students. Some regular education teachers did not understand the interpreting process and described communication as "I would tell the interpreter and the interpreter would tell her" instead of "I would tell her." The lack of ownership became evident in the teacher's inability to gauge the learning of the deaf student. In some instances, it was articulated by the teacher's opinion that "if the deaf student does not understand, it is their fault." Many teachers gave the interpreter full responsibility for monitoring student learning, instead of accepting that responsibility themselves. Another way that lack of ownership was clearly exhibited was by the use of the terminology "them" vs. "us." For example, one teacher noted, "[The deaf students] really didn't talk with us very much."

Another theme that emerged in the responses of the regular education teachers was the need for more education. An example of their knowledge need was found in Eric's quote, "Maybe I'm not a good one to talk to, because I really had no idea what to do with them." While some teachers also recognized their own knowledge need, others seemed to hold fast to myths and used them to guide their interaction with deaf students. Unfortunately, one resource seemed unexpectedly unavailable to them—the deaf education teacher. The regular education teachers in this study reported that they rarely saw the deaf education teachers, and the latter were not involved in supporting them or accommodating for the student's needs.

The final theme that emerged was the teachers' overall willingness to accommodate for the students' needs. However, only two out of four teachers were actively involved in accommodating for the needs of deaf students. Also, none of the teachers reported learning any signs in order to communicate directly with the deaf student. Though the teachers presented a friendly and flexible attitude, in reality, it seemed that the deaf child was expected to adapt to the classroom, not the classroom to the deaf child.

While the themes of language deprivation and social isolation, a lack of ownership, a lack of education, and a willingness to accommodate student's needs emerged as themes in the responses of the regular education teachers' responses, another interesting finding was noted. Each of the regular education teachers approached the deaf student from a very different philosophical standpoint. Therefore, these four teachers seem to represent the distinct approaches of regular education teachers toward their deaf students. The following portrayals were based on the four regular education teacher participants in this study:

Teacher #1 tends to lack basic information about deaf students and their culture. When a deaf student is placed in his class, he tends to ignore the deaf student and focus solely on the hearing students. He sees the deaf student's learning and behavior as solely the responsibility of the interpreter.

On the surface, *Teacher #2* seems accommodating and welcoming to deaf students. He is sensitive to the social needs of deaf students in his classroom, but distances himself from monitoring their learning needs. He makes the interpreter fully responsible for the deaf students, though he may "check in" with her once in a while to see if the deaf student is learning.

Teacher #3 bases her beliefs on a strong stance of equality. She holds the deaf student accountable for their learning and actions, but has a tendency to focus on equality in punitive actions. This teacher bases her actions on the belief that an interpreted education is an equal education and therefore blames the student if a gap in learning occurs. She forces deaf students to high expectations, but shows little compassion and flexibility if they fail.

Teacher #4 takes a reflective role in meeting the needs of the deaf student. Initially this teacher may be nervous about having the deaf student in her class because she feels responsible for the student's learning. She is active in building a collaborative relationship with the interpreter and works with them both inside and outside of class to ensure that the student is learning. She often reflects on her responsibility in meeting the needs of the deaf student, and changes her approach to the deaf student as needed.

11 Conclusions and Recommendations

Deaf student, in a hearing school . . .
How do you feel?
Who do you talk to?
What do you learn?
You live in a box, where
voices are shut out,
and relationships unreachable.
Do you know you are not alone?
You are a part of a rich culture of people.
Smart, Funny, and Talented
You are not alone.

—Representation of an ASL poem by a deaf student

EVERY DAY, DEAF STUDENTS sit in regular education classrooms attempting to access their education. However, they can only gain access to learning and social experiences through an interpreter. This study reaches into the real-life experiences of deaf children and asks, is inclusion an acceptable educational option for deaf children? Does it encourage academic achievement or severely limit deaf children by placing them in an impoverished communicative learning environment, perhaps to detrimental effect? Though many hearing parents would not place their hearing children in a classroom of people who speak a foreign language and give them an interpreter to survive, this is often seen as the viable and best option for deaf children. But is it the best option?

Though deaf educators have long warned of the isolating effects of inclusion (Ross, 1978; Cohen, 1994; Lane, 1992; Nowell, 1997), a high percentage of deaf students remain in inclusive settings. Why? Is there a benefit that has not yet been noted? Peer interaction is widely accepted as playing a significant role in the social and emotional development of children and adolescents (Benard, 1990; Parker, 1993; Krever, 2002), and yet deaf children are consistently placed in communicatively isolated environments. Why?

Federal laws and current educational thinking are moving contrary to the discourse and beliefs of many deaf educational professionals. How does this stark opposition in beliefs and values influence the educational environments of deaf students? Perhaps the responses contained in this study will allow administrators, educators, and policymakers to think more richly and deeply about the multiple perspectives represented, rather than to speak from a bold, one-position stand.

Conclusion

This study invited deaf students to share their opinions of their education environments and to explore the complexities of their perspectives. Then educational interpreters reflected on their own role in the daily experiences of deaf students, as well as their insight into the relationships and communicative interaction that shape deaf students' lives. Deaf education teachers also gave insight into the barriers and underlying belief systems that deaf students face in integrated settings. Finally, regular education teachers shared their views of educating deaf students in their classroom. These multiple perspectives were chosen to give insight into the complexities of the daily experiences of deaf students in integrated educational settings.

In listening to the various voices, the following themes emerged: language deprivation, loneliness and social isolation, and oppression and lack of power. These themes were prevalent in the perspectives of every group of participants.

Language Deprivation

Almost all the participants mentioned that deaf students are deprived of language. This deprivation manifests itself in the lack of interaction with peers, interpreters, teachers, parents, and others. Deaf students shared that very few hearing students learn ASL well enough to hold a conversation, and most of the time they feel frustrated in attempting to communicate with them. Communication between deaf students and their hearing peers was described by interpreters as being shallow, mostly relying on a gesture and pointing system. The regular education teachers had never seen any of the hearing students attempt to learn sign language in order to communicate with the deaf students. Even when an interpreter was available, conversation between hearing students and deaf students was limited to school-related topics. Some interpreters believed this was because of the intrusion of an adult into the conversation. They reported that hearing students might ask deaf students if they finished their homework, but they rarely discussed more intimate topics.

Sadly, when a communication breakdown does occur between a deaf student and a hearing student, the blame is often placed on the deaf student, even though the hearing student is more able to learn sign language than the deaf student is able to learn to speak. This misplaced blame was evident in the opinions of the speaking deaf students, the interpreters, and the regular education teachers. Even worse, as a communication breakdown occurred between deaf signing students and hearing students, it seemed that the deaf signing students themselves felt responsible for the breakdown, which led to feelings of embarrassment and being different. In all, the participants' responses make it clear that hearing students and deaf signing students engage in minimal interaction and minimal relationship building.

Communication between deaf students and their regular education teachers was also described as being quite limited. The regular education teachers believe that the interpreters will monitor the deaf student's behavior and learning, therefore, they may interact with the deaf student to a lesser degree than with their other students. The responses of the deaf students also revealed that they rarely interacted with their regular education teachers and that the teachers often seemed disinterested in learning about their language and their culture.

Even with the interpreter, who is the deaf student's only direct communication partner, the students are often discouraged from having friendly conversations. Instead they are reminded to stay focused on their academic work. The comments of signing deaf students also revealed that an impoverished language environment exists in integrated classrooms. They expressed deep frustrations in trying to build relationships with people who did not share their language.

Loneliness and Social Isolation

Comments about loneliness and social isolation were woven throughout the deaf students' interviews. They seemed to have limited access to the social web of student culture in their schools and did not have a clear understanding of the relationship-building process that is embedded in the term *friend*. Some students shared a sense of cultural isolation, the feeling that their culture and language was neither understood nor valued by anyone in their environment. They felt they were being forced to assimilate with the majority culture, and this gave them a sense of being powerless.

Though hearing peers were usually polite to the deaf students, they rarely engaged in relationship building. Sadly, the deaf students, interpreters, and deaf education teachers all stated that, at the most, only two hearing students learned to sign. Most participants believed that deaf students were limited in choosing friends to the few, if any, students that were willing to learn sign language. As they grew older, the deaf students tended to feel lonelier, as they did not have dating opportunities and often did not spend time with friends outside of school.

Throughout their interviews the deaf students expressed their deep struggle with loneliness and isolation, often linking these feelings to a lack of ability to learn. It seemed that they had an innate understanding of the importance of supporting the social side of learning. One of the students expressed this idea beautifully, "If you don't have anyone to talk with at school and you come home and you don't have anyone to talk to at home then you can get real lonely and just give up. You'll feel like you're not learning anything." This quote is a poignant illustration of Vygotsky's theory that learning awakens a variety of internal developmental processes that are able to operate only when the child is interacting with people in his environment and with his peers (Vygotsky, 1930).

Many of the interpreters and deaf education teachers seemed to be aware of their students' struggle. This loneliness could explain why the deaf students want their interpreters to be more of a friend than a professional. The students believe that the interpreters who are their allies are more effective. The interpreters who agree that a friendship orientation is more effective tend to be actively involved in building social bridges between the deaf students and their hearing peers. These interpreters also seem to understand that many deaf students see the interpreter is an extension of themselves. The extension position contends that the extent to which the interpreter is accepted socially by hearing peers and the regular education teacher directly influences the extent to which the deaf student is accepted.

The interpreters who believe that a professional orientation is more effective are perplexed by the students' strong opinions about what they should or should not wear. They seem to be only minimally aware of their influence on the child's social experiences. Some of the interpreters and other adults in the school focus on the deaf students' academic success rather than their social needs.

Oppression and Lack of Power

The lack of high quality education for deaf students, the promotion of inferiority in deaf students, and the lack of power that is normally afforded to other same-aged students are all evidence of the oppressive nature of integrated schools. The central question all teachers should be asking is, "Are deaf students learning?" The regular education teacher is responsible for monitoring the learning of the students in the class. The teacher asks questions and makes students accountable for the content. However, the deaf students and interpreters in this study reported that the regular education teacher often does not ask the deaf student questions in class and does not make the student accountable for projects and homework. These teachers have low expectations for deaf students and do not expect them to succeed at the same level as hearing students. Unfortunately, when an interpreter accompanies a deaf student into the room, the regular education teacher often expects the interpreter to monitor the deaf student's learning. Curiously, in the interviews with the interpreters, they did not mention that they were aware of this responsibility. Therefore, it seems possible that no one is monitoring the deaf student's learning.

Another indicator of oppression occurs in the classroom when deaf students are made to feel inferior by their peers and teachers. This can occur when deaf students are expected to succeed but are not provided with the necessary support to succeed. The barriers to student success include weak support structures (for example, unqualified interpreters and unqualified interpreter substitutes), deaf education teachers who cannot communicate fluently in ASL, and regular education teachers who do not accommodate for deaf students' needs. The students reported feeling inferior to the hearing students because their teachers had lower expectations for their learning outcomes, they were the victims of bullying, and they were seen as less capable by their peers. Blaming deaf students for communication breakdowns and expecting them to talk (i.e., become more like hearing people, while disregarding their own language and culture) are also forms of oppression.

Many deaf students experience a lack of power within the school. Unlike other students their age, they can not choose their classes and where they want to sit in the classroom. They are often not afforded the power to choose their friends but instead are limited to whoever learns sign language. They are severely limited in their control over their own interactions because they rely heavily on their interpreters. Deaf students are also often limited in their ability to achieve academic success by factors such as the effectiveness of their interpreter, their ability to interact with the curriculum, and the level of support services available. The lack of power that deaf students experience extends far beyond that of other groups of students with disabilities or from those from culturally diverse backgrounds.

Overall, the speaking deaf students find more satisfaction in the social and academic areas of school. They still experience frustrations that lead to feelings of loneliness and isolation, but they do not experience the same level of social isolation as the signing deaf students. However, even the speaking deaf students become frustrated due to the communication barrier. Though it may not be as intense as it is for their signing deaf counterparts, they have moments when they do not understand their teachers and hearing peers, which lead them to feelings of loneliness and of being different. They also express their frustration in being thought of as less capable by peers and teachers. Even the deaf students who have strong speech and hearing skills feel this indicator of oppression.

The speaking deaf students recognize that they are more easily able to access their education through the combined use of an interpreter and their own limited abilities to hear and speak. They know that even these limited abilities greatly increase their capacity to form relationships with hearing peers. At times they relish their role as an intermediary between their deaf and hearing friends. They are proud of their ability to function in two worlds.

The revelations gleaned from this study are consistent with previous studies and the discourse in the field of deaf education. The value of this study is the generation of greater insight into these areas of concern. By probing the perspectives of participants about social interaction and relationship building in integrated educational settings, it contributes to the knowledge base in the field of deaf education. By giving insight into the roles and functions of the educational interpreter, it provides baseline data in areas that were previously unexplored.

While some speaking deaf students are sheltered from the harshest realities of the underlying themes, the signing deaf students feel the full brunt of language deprivation, loneliness, social isolation, and oppression. In some instances, the deaf student's fundamental human rights to language and to education seem to be in danger as they struggle to connect with a hearing world through one channel of access—their interpreter. Therefore, teachers, interpreters, and other school personnel have an obligation to provide deaf students with language-rich environments, opportunities to build relationships with peers, and freedom from oppression.

A majority (64%) of deaf and hard of hearing students are educated in integrated settings (Regional and National Summary Reports, 2005), yet we seem to be functioning in a void of knowledge. A body of research needs to be developed to increase our understanding of the impact of integrated education on the academic achievement of deaf students. Further research is still needed to analyze the technical differences between a direct and an interpreted education. Additionally, there is a critical need to understand the cause-and-effect relationships of longtime language deprivation, loneliness, and social isolation on the mental health of deaf students.

Recommendations

The information gathered in this study has serious implications for federal and state policy makers, school administrators, teacher preparation programs, interpreter preparation programs, and school personnel. To improve the integrated educational experiences of deaf children, I am proposing the following.

Policy at the Federal, State, and District Levels

1. Develop and monitor a national accountability system focusing on the academic achievement of deaf students.

2. Address the knowledge gaps of professionals by creating professional standards for interpreters and teachers who interact with deaf students in different contexts.

3. Develop national educational interpreter certification standards to ensure that all interpreters attain ASL fluency, adhere to a code of ethics, and understand the role of the educational interpreter.

4. Develop state policy to allow students to use ASL credits to meet foreign language requirements.

5. Clearly indicate in both state and local educational policy that schools for deaf students are viable and positive options for deaf students.

6. Enforce the policy of a reverse continuum of least restrictive environments for deaf students so that *least restrictive environment* means that environment yielding the greatest access to language and social learning needs (Department of Education, 1992).

7. Monitor the IEPs of deaf students at the federal level to ensure that the language and communication needs of deaf students are being met.

8. Include a language planning document in each IEP that requires a discussion of how to meet deaf students' language and social learning needs.

9. Create magnet programs for students who choose integrated educational placements to encourage larger numbers of deaf students within the same school.

10. Include in each IEP a plan to identify and service deaf students' mental and emotional health needs with qualified professional providers.

11. Develop policy to provide qualified interpreting substitutes (for example contract with a local interpreting service agency).

Collaboration Between Educational Agencies and Communities

1. Encourage collaboration between state educational agencies, local educational agencies, communities, and religious organizations to create multiple opportunities for deaf students to come together to enhance their language and relationship building.

2. Bring deaf adults into the schools to create cultural connections for deaf students.

Interpreting Programs

1. Revise the curriculum to include instruction on the following topics:

    a) language acquisition of deaf students
    b) educational law and IEP policies
    c) the role of the educational interpreter, including enhancing direct communication between deaf and hearing students
    d) the barriers that deaf students experience in accessing an interpreted education
    e) the social learning needs of all students and the interpreter's role in meeting the social learning needs of deaf students
    f) the deaf student's perspective of an effective educational interpreter

2. Orient future interpreters to their influence on the social experiences of deaf students, such as noted in the "extension theory." This theory posits that the deaf students see the interpreter as an extension of themselves. This theory also suggests that the extent to which the interpreter is accepted socially by hearing students and regular education teachers directly influences the extent to which the deaf student will be accepted.

Support Structures for Educational Interpreters

1. Create an educational interpreting code of ethics to clearly define the ethical standards for educational interpreters.
2. Support higher standards in interpreting through more frequent and spontaneous monitoring of interpreter effectiveness by qualified evaluators.
3. Include a wide variety of professional development options for educational interpreters with a focus on building interpreting skill.

Deaf Education Teacher Preparation Programs

1. Require future teachers to meet a fluency level in American Sign Language before graduating.
2. Include coursework exploring deaf culture, collaborating with interpreters, and managing an educational team.

Regular Education Teacher Preparation Programs

1. Provide basic knowledge about deafness and deaf people and an orientation to the cultural perspective of deafness.
2. Describe the role of regular education teachers with deaf students in their classrooms, including the need to monitor comprehension and to take ownership for meeting the educational and social learning needs of deaf students.
3. Explain the role of the interpreter and the deaf education teacher.
4. Discuss the common accommodations for deaf students in integrated classrooms and the barriers that deaf students face in accessing an education through an interpreter.

Practice in Schools

1. Create a "deaf friendly" environment by ensuring that all auditory information is consistently accessible through visual means, such as closed-captioned videos/DVDs, televisions, CD-ROMS, etc.
2. Empower deaf education teachers to make decisions that support the communication and language needs of deaf students, such as having the flexibility to choose their students' teachers and adjust schedules to place hearing students who sign in the classrooms of deaf students.
3. Ensure that communication is established among the members of the deaf student's educational team, including the educational interpreter.
4. Invite educational interpreters to IEP meetings and encourage them to serve as equal members on the IEP team.
5. Treat the educational interpreter as a professional by ensuring that they have ample planning time, a private and safe place to store resources, and access to appropriate professional development activities.

Professional Development for Teachers, Interpreters, and Other Adults in Schools

Provide professional development for all adults in the school, including administrators, in the cultural perspective of deafness, the basic facts concerning deafness, and culturally competent methods of communicating with deaf individuals.

Policy for Addressing Mental Health Needs

1. Establish a plan to assess deaf students' mental and emotional health needs.
2. Contract with psychologists or counselors skilled in ASL who can meet the mental health needs of deaf students directly, rather than through interpreters.

The voices of deaf children, as well as their interpreters and teachers, paint a picture of deprivation of communication and deprivation of social contacts. But our ceaseless worrying about the academic achievement of deaf children has not enacted change. By moving these recommendations into action, support structures are created to increase the language and social experiences of deaf children. By doing so, we can make a positive impact on the lives of children and their future academic success.

References

Adorno, T. (1974). *Minima moralia: Reflections from a damaged life*. London: New Left Books.

Afzali-Nomani, E. (1995). Educational conditions related to successful full inclusion programs involving deaf/hard of hearing children. *American Annals of the Deaf, 140*(2), 396–401.

Anderson, T., & Soden, R. (2001). Peer interaction and the learning of critical thinking skills. *Pschology Learning and Teaching, 1*(1), 37–40.

Antia, S. (1982). Social interaction of partially mainstreamed hearing-impaired children. *American Annals of the Deaf, 137*, 381–388.

Antia, S., & Kreimeyer, K. (2001). The role of interpreters in inclusive classrooms. *American Annals of the Deaf, 146*(4), 31–38.

Antia, S., & Stinson, M. (2002). Developing membership in the education of deaf and hard-of-hearing students in inclusive settings. *Journal of Deaf Studies and Deaf Education, 7*(3).

Arnold, P. (1984). The education of the deaf child: Integration or autonomy? *American Annals of the Deaf, 129*(1), 29–37.

Asidao, C, Vion, S., & Espelage, D. L. (1999, August 21). *Interviews with middle school students*. Champaign, IL: ERIC Clearinghouse on Elementary and Early Childhood Education

Aymard, L., & Winstanley, C. (1992). *Reflections on the language and culture of deaf Americans*. Dubuque, Iowa: Kendall Hunt.

Baker, C. (2003). Personal interview. In J. Cerney (Ed.).

Banks, J. (1994). *All of us together: The story of inclusion at the Kinzie School*. Washington, D.C.: Gallaudet University Press.

Barton. (1977). The educational environment. In J. Davis (Ed.), *Our forgotten children: Hard of hearing children in schools*. Minneapolis: Self Help for Hard of Hearing People.

Bat-Chava, Y. (2000). Diversity of deaf identities. *American Annals of the Deaf, 145*(5), 420–427.

Bat-Chava, Y., & Deignan, E. (2001). Peer relationships of children with cochlear implants. *Journal of Deaf Studies and Deaf Education, 6*(3).

Bell, N., Grossen, M., & Perret-Clermont, A. (1995). Sociocognitive conflict and intellectual growth. In M. W. Berkowitz (Ed.), *New directions for child development* (No. 29, pp. 41–54). San Francisco: Jossey-Bass.

Benard, B. (1990). *A case for peers.* Portland, OR: Northwest Regional Educational Laboratory.

Block, M. (1999). Have we jumped on the wrong bandwagon? *Palaestra, 15*(3).

Bly, R. (1996). *The sibling society.* New York: Vintage Books.

Boyd, V. (1992). *School Context: Bridge or Barrier to Change.* Austin: Southwest Educational Development Laboratory.

Bremner, A. (1996). *Issues in educational settings for deaf students and interpreters.* Melbourne: Victoria University.

Brown, D. (1999). *Improving academic achievement: What school counselors can do*: Washington, D.C.: U.S. Department of Education Office of Educational Research and Improvement.

Brown, S. E. (1996, August). We are who we are . . . so who are we? *Mainstream Magazine.*

Brueggemann, B. (1995). The coming out of Deaf culture and American Sign Language: An exploration into visual rhetoric and literacy. *Rhetoric Review, 13*(2).

Bulach, C., Brown, C., & Potter, L. (1998). Behaviors that create a caring learning community. *Journal of a Just and Caring Education, 4*(4), 458–470.

Bunch, G. (1994). An interpretation of full inclusion. *American Annals of the Deaf, 139*(2), 150–152.

Burch, D. (2002) Essential education for sign language interpreters in pre-college educational settings, *Journal of Interpretation*: Alexandria, VA.

Burch, D. (2005) Essential language/system competencies for sign language interpreters in pre-college educational settings, *Journal of Interpretation*: Alexandria, VA.

Byrk, A. S., & Schneider, B. (2002). *Trust in schools.* New York: Russell Sage Foundation.

Cambra, C. (2002). Acceptance of deaf students by hearing students in regular classrooms. *American Annals of the Deaf, 147*(1), 38–45.

Cawthon, S. (2005, April) The impact of accountability reform on assessment practices for deaf and hard of hearing students, *American Educational Research Association*, Montreal, Canada.

Center for Disease Control. (2003). What is EHDI? National Center for Birth Defects and Developmental Disabilities, Early Hearing Detection and Intervention Program, U.S. Department of Health and Human Services. Retrieved from www.cdc.gov/ncbddd/ehdi/ehdi.htm.

Cerney, B. (2004). *Relayed interpretations from English to American Sign Language via a hearing and a deaf interpreter*, Unpublished manuscript.

Cerney, B. (2005). *The Interpreting Handbook*, Colorado Springs, CO: Hand and Mind.

Chafin Seal, B. (1998). *Best practices in educational interpreting*. Needham Heights, MA: Allyn and Bacon.

Chen, X., Rubin, K. H., & Li, D. (1997). Relation between academic achievement and social adjustment: Evidence from Chinese children. *Developmental Psychology, 33*, 518–525.

Cohen, O. (1994a). An administrator's view on inclusion for deaf children. *American Annals of the Deaf, 139*(2), 159–161.

Cohen, O. (1994b). "Inclusion" should not include deaf students. *Education Week, 13*(30).

Cohen, O. (1994c). Introduction. In R. C. Johnson & O. Cohen (Eds.), *Implications and complications for Deaf students of the full inclusion movement* (pp. 1–88). Washington, D.C.: Gallaudet Research Institute and Conference of Educational Administrators Serving the Deaf.

Cokely, D. (1992). The effects of lag time of interpreting errors. In D. Cokely (Ed.), *Sign Language Interpreters and Interpreting* (pp. 39–69). Burtonsville, MD: Linstok.

Coleman, J. (1966), *Equality of Educational Opportunity*. Washington, D.C.: United States Government Printing Office, 21–22.

Cooper, D., & Snell, J. (2003). Bullying—not just a kid thing. *Educational Leadership, 66*(6), 22–25.

Cromwell, S. (1997). "Inclusion: Has it gone too far?" *Education World*. Retrieved October 31, 2003, from http://www.education-world.com/a_curr/curr034.shtml

Curtiss, S. (1977). *Genie: A psycholinguistic study of a modern-day "wild-child."* New York: Academic Press.

Dahl, C., & Wilcox, S. (1990). Preparing the educational interpreter: A survey of sign language interpreter training programs. *American Annals of the Deaf, 135*(4), 275–279.

Deiro, J. (2003). Do your students know you care? *Educational Leadership, 60*(6), 60–62.

Denbo, S., Grant, C., & Jackson, S. (2001). *EDUCATE AMERICA: A Call for Equity in School Reform*. Portland, OR: American Youth Policy Forum, Mid-Atlantic Equity Consortium.

Evans, J. (1998). Changing the lens: A position paper on the value of qualitative research methodology as a mode of inquiry in the education of the deaf. *American Annals of the Deaf, 143*(2), 246–254.

Ferreira, M., Smith, G., & Bosworth, K. (2002). Critical dimensions of the caring culture of an urban middle school. *International Electronic Journal for Leadership in Learning, 6*(3).

Feshbach, N., & Feshbach, S. (1987). Affective processes and academic achievement. *Child Development*, 1149–1156.

Forman, E. A., & Kraker, M. J. (1985, September). The social origins of logic: The contributions of Piaget and Vygotsky. *New Directions for Child Development, 29*, 23–39.

Foster, S. (1988). Life in the mainstream: Reflections of deaf college freshmen on their experiences in the mainstreamed high school. *Journal of Rehabilitation of the Deaf, 22*(2), 27–35.

Frey, K. (2002). *New Insights into Special Education*. Paper presented at the 2002 Office of Special Education Programs Research Project Directors' Meeting, Washington D.C.

Gallaudet, E. (1992). The value of the sign-language to the deaf. In L. Aymard & W. C. (Eds.), *Reflections on the language and culture of deaf Americans*. Dubuque, Iowa: Kendall Hunt.

Gallaudet Research Institute (January, 2005). *Regional and national summary report of data from the 2003–2004 Annual Survey of Deaf and Hard of Hearing Children & Youth*. Washington, D.C.: GRI, Gallaudet University.

Gannon, J. (1981). *Deaf heritage: A narrative history of Deaf America*. Silver Spring, MD: National Association of the Deaf.

Giangreco, M. (2003). Working with paraprofessionals. *Educational Leadership, 61*(2), 50–53.

Goldhaber, D., Anthony, E. (2004, March 8) Can teacher quality be effectively assessed? *Urban Institute*. Retrieved from http://www.urban.org/url.cfm?ID=410958

Griffith, P. L., Johnson, H. A., & Dastoli, S. L. (1985). If teaching is conversation, can conversation be taught? Discourse abilities in hearing-impaired children. In D. N. Ripich & F. M. Spinelli (Eds.), *School discourse problems* (pp. 149–177). San Deigo, CA: College-Hill Press.

Gustason, G. (1985). Interpreters entering public school employment. *American Annals of the Deaf, 130*(4), 265–266.

Halpern, C. (1996). Listening in on Deaf culture. *Standards, 5*(2).

Hanson, D. (2003). *No Child Left Behind: What will it take?* Paper presented at the CEASD National Conference, Sioux Falls, SD.

Harris, J. (1995). *The cultural meaning of deafness.* Brookfield, VT: Ashgate.

Harvey, M. (2003). Shielding yourself from the perils of empathy: The case of sign language interpreters. *Journal of Deaf Studies and Deaf Education, 8*(2), 207–213.

Hayes, P. L. (1992). Educational interpreters for deaf students: Their responsibilities, problems, and concerns. *RID Journal of Interpretation, 5,* 5–24.

Hoffman, D., & Levak, B. (2003). Personalizing schools. *Educational Leadership, 61*(1), 30–34.

Holt, J., Traxler, C., & Allen, T. (1997). *Interpreting the scores: A user's guide to the 9th edition Stanford Achievement Test for educators of deaf and hard-of-hearing students.* Washington, D.C.: Gallaudet University.

Hoshaurer, L. (1991). *Deaf Life, 5*(November).

Humphrey, J., & Alcorn, B. (1995). *So you want to be an interpreter.* Amarillo, TX: H&H.

Humphries, T., Padden, C., & O'Rourke, T. (1994). *A basic course in American Sign Language.* Silver Spring, MD: T. J.

Jimenez-Sanchez, C., & Antia, S. (1999). Team-teaching in an integrated classroom: Perceptions of deaf and hearing teachers. *Journal of Deaf Studies and Deaf Education, 4,* 215–224.

John-Steiner, V., & Mahn, H. (1996). Sociocultural approaches to learning and development: A Vygotskian framework. *Educational Psychologist, 31*(3/4).

Johnson, R., Liddell, S., & Erting, C. (1989). *Unlocking the curriculum: Principles for achieving access in deaf education.* Washington D.C.: Gallaudet Research Institute.

Jones, B. (1999). Providing access: "New roles for educational interpreters". *RID Views, 16*(2), 15.

Jones, B., Clark, G., & Soltz, D. (1997). Characteristics and practices of sign language interpreters in inclusive education programs. *Exceptional Children, 63*(2), 257–268.

Karchmer, M., & Allen, T. (1999). The functional assessment of deaf and hard of hearing students. *American Annals of the Deaf, 144*(2), 68–77.

Kauffman, J., & Hallahan, D. (Eds.), (1995). *The illusion of full inclusion: A comprehensive critique of a current special education bandwagon.* Austin, TX: Pro-Ed.

Kluwin, T. (1999). Coteaching deaf and hearing students: Research on social integration. *American Annals of the Deaf, 144*(4), 339–344.

Kluwin, T., & Stewart, D. (2001, Spring). Interpreting in schools—A look at research. *Odyssey, 2*(2).

Kluwin, T., & Stinson, M. (1993). *Deaf students in local public high schools.* Springfield, IL: Charles C. Thomas.

Knight, P., & Swanwick, R. (1997). Inclusion of deaf children in mainstream education. *The Regional Review.*

Kreimeyer, K., Crooke, P., Drye, C., Egbert, V., & Klein, B. (2000). Academic and social benefits of a co-enrollment model of inclusive education for deaf and hard-of-hearing children. *Journal of Deaf Studies and Deaf Education, 5*(2).

Krever, E. M. (2002). *Peer relations of mainstreamed hearing impaired students.* University of Toronto, Toronto.

La Pointe, S. (1997). Educational interpreting: The misunderstood profession. *RID Views, 14*(3).

Lane, H. (1992). *The mask of benevolence.* New York: Alfred A. Knopf.

Lane, H. (1993). Cochlear implants; Their cultural and historical meaning. In J. V. Van Cleve (Ed.), *Deaf history unveiled* (pp. 272–291). Washington D.C.: Gallaudet University Press.

Lane, H., Hoffmeister, R., & Bahan, B. (2002). Educational placement and the deaf child. In M. A. Byrnes (Ed.), *Taking sides: Clashing views of controversy in special education.* Boston: McGraw-Hill.

Lang, H. G., F. J. Dowaliby, & Anderson, H. (1994). Critical teaching incidents: Recollections of deaf college students. *American Annals of the Deaf, 139(2)*, 119–127.

LeFever, G., Dawson, K., & Morrow, A. (1999, September). The extent of drug therapy for attention-deficit/hyperactivity disorder among children in public school. *American Journal of Public Health, 89*, 1359–1364.

Leigh, I. (1994). Psychosocial implications of full inclusion for deaf children and adolescents. In R. C. Johnson & O. Cohen (Eds.), *Implications and complications for deaf students of the full inclusion movement.* Washington, D.C.: Gallaudet Research Institute and Conference of Educational Administrators Serving the Deaf.

Lloyd-Jones, G. (2003). Design and control issues in qualitative case study research. *International Journal of Qualitative Methods, 2*(2).

Loizou, P. C. (1998, September). Introduction to cochlear implants. *IEEE Signal Processing Magazine, 15*(5), 101–130.

Luckner, J. L., & Muir, S. (2001). Successful students who are deaf in general education. *American Annals of the Deaf, 146*(5), 435–445.

Luckner, J. L., Muir, G., Howell, J., Sebald, A., & Young, J. (2005). An examination of the research and training needs in the field of deaf education *American Annals of the Deaf, 150*(4), 358–368.

Malever, M., & Safer, D. (2000). Stimulant treatment in Maryland Public Schools. *Pediatrics, 106*(3), 533–539.

Marschark, M., Lang, H., & Albertini, J. (2002). *Educating deaf students: From research to practice.* New York: Oxford University Press.

Marschark, M., & Spencer, P. (2003). *Oxford handbook of deaf studies, language, and education.* New York: Oxford University Press.

McCartney, B. (1994). Inclusion as a practical matter. *American Annals of the Deaf, 139*(2), 161–162.

McCrone, W. (2004, Spring). School bullying a problem for deaf and hard of hearing students, *Odyssey, 5*(2), 6–9.

Meadow-Orlans, K. P., Mertens, D., & Sass-Lehrer, M. (2003). Hard of hearing children: Still overlooked. *Odyssey, 4*(2), 4–9.

Mendes, E. (2003). What empathy can do. *Educational Leadership, 61*(1), 56–59.

Mertens, D. (1989). Social experiences of hearing-impaired high school youth. *American Annals of the Deaf, 134*(1), 15–19.

Meyer, K. (2003). In class hard of hearing children face misunderstanding. *Odyssey, 4*(2), 18–21.

Mills, J. (1996). Educational interpreting at the elementary level. *RID Views, 13*(3).

Mitchell, R., & Karchmer, M. (2006). Demographics of deaf education: more students in more places. *American Annals of the Deaf, 151*(2), 95–104.

Moore, M., & Livitan, L. (1993). Deaf and dumb. In *For hearing people only.* Rochester, NY: MSM Productions.

Moxley, A., & Loggins, S. (1991, Winter). Learning disabilities in deaf and hard of hearing children. *Endeavor,* 18–20.

Mudgett-DeCaro. (1997). Classroom dialogues and Deaf identities. *American Annals of the Deaf, 142*(2), 96–99.

Murphy, R. (1995). Encounters: The body silent in America. In B. Ingstad & S. Whyte (Eds.), *Disability and culture.* Berkeley, CA: University of California Press.

National Center for Hearing Assessment and Management (2003). *State summary statistics: Universal newborn hearing screening.* Logan, UT: Utah State University.

National Dissemination Center for Children with Disabilities. (1998). The history of the idea. Retrieved from http://www.nichcy.org/idea.htm

National Center on Deafness. (2002). Language experience/exposure. In *Preparing postsecondary professionals*. Northridge, California State University. Retrieved from http://p3.csun.edu/p3access/mod-litread.html

Newport, E. (2001). *Critical periods in the acquisition of language*. Paper presented at the Symposium: Critical Periods in Language Development, Chicago.

Nover, S. (1995). Full inclusion for deaf students: An ethnographic perspective. In B. Snider (Ed.), *Inclusion? Defining quality education for deaf and hard of hearing students*. Washington, D.C.: Gallaudet University.

Nussbaum, D. (2003). *Cochlear implants: Navigating a forest of information . . . one tree at a time*. Retrieved Jan. 14, 2004, from http://clerccenter.gallaudet. edu/KidsWorldDeafNet/e-docs/CI/index.html

Olweus, D. (2003). A profile of bullying at school. *Educational Leadership, 60*(6), 12–17.

Oral Deaf Education (2003). *Oral Deaf Education Library*. Alexander Graham Bell Association, Retrieved November 9, 2003, from www.oraldeafed.org

OSERS 23rd report to congress on the implementation of the IDEA. (2002). Office of Special Education.

Osman, B. (1982). *No one to play with: The social side of learning*. New York: Random House.

Osterman, K. (2000). Students' need for belonging in the school community. *Review of Educational Research, 70*(3), 323–367.

Padden, C., & Humphries, T. (1988). *Deaf In America: Voices from a Culture*. Cambridge, MA: Harvard University Press.

Palinscsar, A. S. (1998). Social constructivist perspectives on teaching and learning. *Annual Review of Psychology, 49*, 345–375.

Patrie, C. (1994). Educational interpreting: Who leads the way? *RID Views, 11*(2).

Percentage of students ages 6 through 21 with disabilities served in different educational environments. (2003). U.S. Department of Education, Office of Special Education Programs, Data Analysis Systems. Retrieved August 28, 2007, from www.allcountries.org/uscensus/281_children_and_youth_with_disabilities_served.html

Piaget, J. (1985). *The Equilibration of cognitive structures: The central problem of intellectual development*. Chicago: University of Chicago Press.

Powers, S. (2003). Influences of student and family factors on academic outcomes of mainstream secondary school deaf students. *Journal of Deaf Studies and Deaf Education, 8*(1), 57–74.

Preparing Postsecondary Professionals Project. (2003). Language experience/exposure. California State University, Northridge. Retrieved from http://p3.csun.edu/p3access/mod-litread.html

President's Commission on Excellence in Special Education (2002). *A New Era: Revitalizing Special Education for Children and Their Families.* Washington D.C.: U.S. Department of Education.

Preventing Bullying: A Manual for Schools and Communities. (1998). US Department of Education.

Rafferty, Y., Piscitelli, V., & Boettcher, C. (2003). The Impact of language development and social competence among preschooler with disabilities. *Exceptional Children, 69*(4).

Ragizzino, K., Resnik, H., Utne-O'Brien, M., & Weissberg, R. (2003, Summer). Promoting academic achievement through social and emotional learning. *Educational Horizons,* 169–171.

Ramsey, C. (1994). The price of dreams: Who will pay it? In R. C. Johnson & O. Cohen (Eds.), *Implications and complications for deaf students of the full inclusion movement.* Washington, D.C.: Gallaudet Research Institute and Conference of Educational Administrators Serving the Deaf.

Ramsey, C. (1997). Deaf children in public schools: Placement, context, and consequences. Washington, D.C.: Gallaudet University Press.

Regional and national summary report of data from the 2004–2005 annual survey of deaf and hard of hearing children & youth. (2005, December). Washington D.C.: Gallaudet Research Institute.

Resnick, L. B., Salmon, M. H., Zeitz, C. M., Wahter, S. H., and Holowchak, M. (1993). Reasoning in conversation. *Cognition and Instruction, 11,* 347–364.

Rice, J. K. (2003) *Teacher quality: Understanding the effectiveness of teacher attributes.* Washington, D.C.: Economic Policy Institute.

Roach, A. (2002). Empowering the young Deaf community. *RID Views, 19*(3).

Ross, M. (1978). Mainstreaming: Some social considerations. *Volta Review* (January), 21–30.

Roy, C. (1989). *A sociolinguistic analysis of the interpreter's role in the turn exchanges of an interpreted event.* PhD diss., Georgetown University, Washington, D.C.

Roy, C. (1992). A sociolinguistic analysis of the interpreter's role in simultaneous talk in face-to-face interpreted dialogue. *Sign Language Studies, 74,* 21–61.

Rubin, H., & Rubin, I. (1995). *Qualitative interviewing: The art of hearing data.* London: Sage Publications.

Runkel, P. (1990). *Casting nets and testing specimens: Grand methods of psychology.* New York: Praeger.

Rutherford, S. (1983). Funny in Deaf—not in hearing. *Journal of American Folklore, 96,* 381.

Sacks, O. (1989). *Seeing voices: A journey into a deaf world.* Berkeley, CA: University of California Press.

Sapon-Shevin, M. (2003). Inclusion: A matter of social justice. *Educational Leadership, 61*(2), 25–28.

Sass-Lehrer, M., Gerner de Garcia, B., & Rovins, M. (1997). *Creating a multicultural school climate for deaf children and their families.* Washington D.C.: Gallaudet University: Laurent Clerc National Deaf Education Center.

Saur, R. E., Layne, C., Hurley, E., & Opton, K. (1986). Dimensions of mainstreaming. *American Annals of the Deaf, 131*(5), 325–329.

Schick, B., & Williams, K. (2003, January 7). *What is the EIPA?* Retrieved January 23, 2004, from http://spot.colorado.edu/~schick/EIPAWT_about.html

Schick, B., Williams, K., & Bolster, L. (1999). Skill levels of educational interpreters working in public schools. *Journal of Deaf Studies and Deaf Education, 4,* 144–155.

Schildroth, A., & Hotto, S. (1997). Deaf students and full inclusion: Who wants to be excluded? In R. C. Johnson & O. Cohen (Eds.), *Implications and complications for deaf students of the full inclusion movement.* Washington, D.C.: Gallaudet Research Institute and Conference of Educational Administrators Serving the Deaf.

Schloss, P., Selinger, J., Goldsmith, L., & Morrow, L. (1983). Classroom-based approaches to developing social competence among hearing-impaired youth. *American Annals of the Deaf, 128*(6), 842–849.

Siegel, L. (2000). The educational & communication needs of deaf and hard of hearing children: A statement of principle on fundamental educational change. *American Annals of the Deaf, 145*(2), 64–77.

Shaw, J., & Jamieson, J. (1995). Interactions of an integrated child with his hearing partners: A Vygotskian perspective. *ACEHI Journal, 21*(1), 4–9.

Shaw, J., & Jamieson, J. (1997). Patterns of classroom discourse in an integrated, interpreted elementary school setting. *American Annals of the Deaf, 142*(2), 40–47.

Sheridan, M. (2001). Inner Lives of Deaf Children: Interviews & Analysis. Washington D.C.: Gallaudet University Press.

Silver, N. (2003). When one size doesn't fit one! *Odyssey, 4*(2), 24–27.

Stake, R. (1995). *The art of case study.* Thousand Oaks, CA: Sage.

Stewart, D., & Stinson, M. (1992).The role of sport and extracurricular activities in shaping socialization patterns. In T. Kluwin, D. Moores & M. Gonter-Gaustad

(Eds.), *Toward effective public school programs for deaf students: Context, process, and outcomes.* New York: Teacher's College Press.

Stinson, M., & Lang, H. (1994a). Full inclusion: A path for integration or isolation? *American Annals of the Deaf, 139*(2), 156–158.

Stinson, M., & Lang, H. (1994b). The potential impact on deaf students of the full inclusion movement. In R. C. Johnson & O. Cohen (Eds.), *Implications and complications for deaf students of the full inclusion movement.* Washington, D.C.: Gallaudet Research Institute and Conference of Educational Administrators Serving the Deaf.

Stinson, M., & Whitmire, K. (1992a). Students' views of their social relationships. In T. Kluwin, D. Moores & M. Gonter Gaustad, (Eds.), *Toward effective public school programs for deaf students: Context, Process and outcomes.* New York: Teacher's College Press.

Stone, R. (1994). Mainstreaming and inclusion: A Deaf perspective. In R. C. Johnson & O. Cohen (Eds.), *Implications and complications for deaf students of the full inclusion movement.* Washington, D.C.: Gallaudet Research Institute and Conference of Educational Administrators Serving the Deaf.

Strong, R., Silver, H., Perini, M., & Tuculesco, G. (2003). Boredom, and its opposite. *Educational Leadership, 61*(1).

Students with emotional disturbance. (2000). Washington D.C.: Center for Effective Collaboration and Practice.

Taylor, M. (1993). *Interpretation skills: English to American Sign Language.* Alberta, Canada: Interpreting Consolidated.

Taylor, M. (2002). *Interpretation skills: American Sign Language to English.* Alberta, Canada: Interpreting Consolidated.

Tucker, J. E. (2004). Language role models and ping pong. *The Maryland Bulletin, 124*(1), 13.

U. S. Census Bureau (1997). Disability status of children under 15 years old.

U.S. Department of Education (1992). *Deaf students education services: Policy guidance.* Washington D.C.: Office for Civil Rights.

U.S. Department of Education. (2001). Public Law print of PL 107-110, No Child Left Behind Act of 2001. Retrieved from http://www.ed.gov/policy/elsec/leg/esea02/index.html

U.S. Department of Education. (2002). Children and youth with disabilities served by selected programs.

Valli, C., & Lucas, C. (1995). *Linguistics of American Sign Language: An introduction.* Washington, D.C.: Gallaudet University Press.

Van Cleve, J. V. (Ed.). (1993). *Deaf history unveiled*. Washington D.C.: Gallaudet University Press.

Van Cleve, J. V., & Crouch, B. (1989). *A place of their own*. Washington D.C.: Gallaudet University Press.

Vandell, D. L., & George, L. B. (1981). Social Interaction in hearing and deaf preschoolers: Successes and failures in initiations. *Child Development, 52*, 627–635.

Vesey, K., & Wilson, B. (2003). Navigating the hearing classroom with a hearing loss. *Odyssey, 4*(5), 10–13.

Villa, R., & Thousand, J. (2003). Making inclusive education work. *Educational Leadership, 61*(2), 19–23.

Voss, J. F., Wiley, J., & Carretero, M. (1995). Acquiring intellectual skills. *Annual Review of Psychology, 46*, 155–181.

Vygotsky, L. S. (1978). *Mind in society: The development of higher psychological processes*. Cambridge, MA: Harvard University Press.

Weiner, J. (2002). A multisource exploration of the friendship patterns of children with and without learning disabilities. *Journal of Abnormal Psychology, 9*.

Weissberg, R., Resnik, H., Payton, J., & O'Brien, M. (2003). Evaluating social and emotional learning programs. *Educational Leadership, 60*(6), 46–50.

Wells, M. (2002). Falls City Schools sued for bullying under Americans with Disabilities Act. National Public Radio Network, Nebraska Educational Telecommunications, Lincoln, NE.

Wilson, C. (1997). Mainstream or "Deaf School?" *Perspectives in Education and Deafness, 16*(2).

Winston, E. (1994a). An interpreted education: inclusion or exclusion? In R. C. Johnson & O. P. Cohen (Eds.), *Implications and complications for deaf students of the full inclusion movement* (pp. 55–62). Washington D.C.: Gallaudet Research Institute and Conference of Educational Administrators Serving the Deaf.

Winston, E. (1998). Ethics in educational interpreting. *RID Views, 15*(2), 30–32.

Wixtrom, C. (1992). Two views of deafness. In L. Aymard & C. Winstonley (Eds.), *Reflections on the language and culture of Deaf Americans*. Dubuque, Iowa: Kendall Hunt.

Yarger, C. (2001). Educational interpreting: Understanding the rural experience. *American Annals of the Deaf, 146*(1), 16–30.

Yin, R. K. (1994). *Case study research: Design and methods*. Thousand Oaks, CA: Sage.

Yoshinaga-Itano, C., & Apuzzo, M. L. (1998). Identification of hearing loss after age 18 months is not early enough. *American Annals of the Deaf, 143*(2), 380–381.

Zapien, C. (1998). Options in deaf education—history, methodologies, and strategies for surviving the system. *Exceptional Parent Magazine* (September).

Index

The letter "f" following a page number denotes a figure.
The letter "t" following a page number denotes a table.